FLAGSHIP HISTORYMAKERS

ELIZABETH I

NICHOLAS FELLOWS

ns

⸱ A⸱ ⸱ ⸱ ⸱ ⸱ ⸱ers

Published by HarperCollins*Publishers* Ltd
77–85 Fulham Palace Road
London
W6 8JB

© HarperCollins*Publishers* Ltd 2004
First published 2004

10 9 8 7 6 5 4 3 2 1

ISBN 000 717316 4

British Library Cataloguing in Publication Data. A
catalogue record for this book is available from the
British Library.

Series commissioned by Graham Bradbury
Project management by Will Chuter
Edited by Hilary Quantrill and Antonia Maxwell
Cover and book design by Derek Lee
Picture research by Celia Dearing
Production by Sarah Robinson
Printed and bound by Scotprint

ACKNOWLEDGEMENTS

The Publishers would like to thank the following for
permission to reproduce extracts from their books:

Macmillan for extract from *The Reign of Elizabeth I*
(1984) ed. Christopher Haigh. Longman for extract
from *Elizabeth I* (1988) by Christopher Haigh.

The Publishers would like to thank the following
for permission to reproduce pictures on these pages
T=Top, B=Bottom, L=Left, R=Right, C=Centre

www.bridgeman.co.uk/Prado Madrid, Philip II of
Spain 1565 (oil on canvas) by Sofonisba Anguisciola
10, www.bridgeman.co.uk/ Musée Conde,
Chantilly/Lauros/Giraudon Duke of Anjou French
School (oil on panel) 20T,
www.bridgeman.co.uk/Musée des Beaux-
Arts/Lauros/Giraudon Charles V (oil on canvas) by
Christoph Amberger 22,
www.bridgeman.co.uk/Rochdale Art Gallery,
Lancashire, Duke of Alençon (oil on panel) by
Francois Clouet 20B,
www.bridgeman.co.uk/Kunsthistorisches Museum,
Vienna Sir Francis Drake 1581 by Nicholas Hilliard
23L,www.bridgeman.co.uk/Private Collection/The
Stapleton Collection 23R,
www.bridgeman.co.uk/Private Collection Elizabeth
I Armada portrait *c*.1588 (oil on panel) English
School 26, www.bridgeman.co.uk/Palazzo
Barberini, Rome Erasmus of Rotterdam (oil on
canvas)by Quentin Massys or Metsys 33,
www.bridgeman.co.uk/Private Collection 54; by
courtesy of the Marquess of Salisbury, Rainbow
portrait of Elizabeth I 1600–1603 attributed to
Marcus Gheeraerts the Younger 50; Mary Evans
Picture Library 24T, 35, 40, 41, 42, Mary Evans
Picture Library/Douglas McCarthy 13; National
Portrait Gallery, London: The Coronation portrait
of Elizabeth I *c*.1600 (oil on panel) by an unknown
artist 7, Mary I 1544 (oil on panel) by Hans Eworth
8, Edward VI 1547 (oil on panel) by unknown artist
9, Mary, Queen of Scots *c*.1560–1565 (oil on panel)
by unknown artist 12, Robert Dudley, Earl of
Leicester 1576 (watercolour on vellum) by Nicholas
Hilliard 24B, Sir Francis Walsingham *c*.1587 (oil on
panel) by John de Critz 37, William Cecil, 1st Baron
Burghley after 1572 (oil on panel) by unknown
artist 48, Thomas Howard, 4th Duke of Norfolk (oil
on panel) by unknown artist 57.

Cover picture: Elizabeth I Armada portrait *c*.1588
(oil on panel) English School,
www.bridgeman.co.uk/Private Collection

Contents

Why do historians differ?

THE purpose of the Flagship Historymakers series is to explore the main debates surrounding a number of key individuals in British, European and American History.

Each book begins with a chronology of the significant events in the life of the particular individual, and an outline of the person's career. The book then examines in greater detail three of the most important and controversial issues in the life of the individual – issues which continue to attract differing views from historians, and which feature prominently in examination syllabuses in A level History and beyond.

Each of these issue sections provides students with an overview of the main arguments put forward by historians. By posing key questions, these sections aim to help students to think through the areas of debate and to form their own judgements on the evidence. It is important, therefore, for students to understand why historians differ in their views on past events and, in particular, on the role of individuals in past events.

The study of History is an ongoing debate about events in the past. Although factual evidence is the essential ingredient of history, it is the *interpretation* of factual evidence that forms the basis for historical debate. The study of how and why historians differ in their various interpretations is termed 'historiography'.

Historical debate can occur for a wide variety of reasons:

Insufficient evidence

In some cases there is insufficient evidence to provide a definitive conclusion. In attempting to 'fill the gaps' where factual evidence is unavailable, historians use their professional judgement to make 'informed comments' about the past.

New evidence

As new evidence comes to light, an historian today may have more information on which to base judgements than historians in the past. For instance, a major source of information explaining Philip II's attitude towards the government of Spain was discovered recently in a back street of Madrid, being used as toilet paper! It is only recently that historians have started to assess this evidence and alter their views accordingly.

A 'philosophy' of history?

Many historians have a specific view of history that will affect the way they make their historical judgements. For instance, Marxist historians – who take their view from the writings of Karl Marx, the founder of modern socialism – believe that society has always been made up of competing economic and social classes. They also place considerable importance on economic reasons behind human decision-making. Therefore, a Marxist historian looking at an historical issue may take a completely different viewpoint to a non-Marxist historian.

The role of the individual

Some historians have seen history as being largely moulded by the acts of specific individuals. Henry VIII, Mary Tudor and Elizabeth I are seen as individuals whose personality and beliefs changed the course of sixteenth-century English history. Other historians have tended to play down the roles of individuals; instead, they highlight the importance of more general social, religious, economic and political change. They tend to see the political and religious changes of the sixteenth century as being caused by a broader group of individuals. An example of this might be the emerging gentry class, which was gaining its wealth from the religious changes and began to demand a greater role in government.

Placing different emphasis on the same historical evidence

Even if historians do not possess different philosophies of history or place different emphasis on the role of the individual, it is still possible for them to disagree in one very important way. This is that they may place different emphases on aspects of the same factual evidence. As a result, History should be seen as a subject that encourages debate about the past, based on historical evidence.

Historians will always differ

Historical debate is, in its nature, continuous. What today may be an accepted view about a past event may well change in the future, as the debate continues.

Timeline: Elizabeth I's life

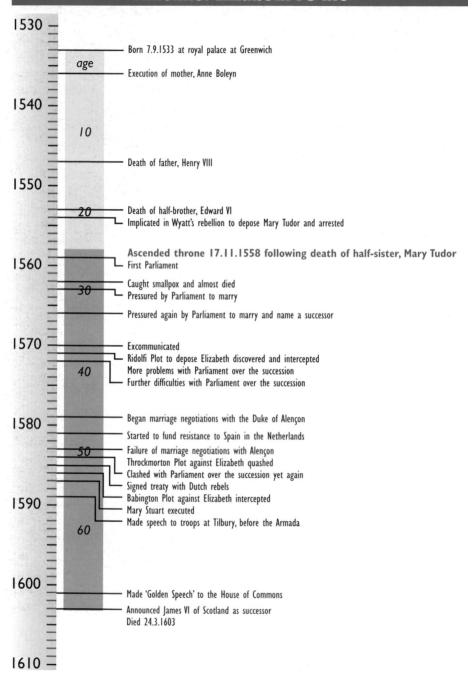

Year		Event

1530

— Born 7.9.1533 at royal palace at Greenwich

age

— Execution of mother, Anne Boleyn

1540

10

— Death of father, Henry VIII

1550

20 — Death of half-brother, Edward VI
— Implicated in Wyatt's rebellion to depose Mary Tudor and arrested

Ascended throne 17.11.1558 following death of half-sister, Mary Tudor
1560 — First Parliament

— Caught smallpox and almost died
30 — Pressured by Parliament to marry

— Pressured again by Parliament to marry and name a successor

1570 — Excommunicated
— Ridolfi Plot to depose Elizabeth discovered and intercepted
40 — More problems with Parliament over the succession
— Further difficulties with Parliament over the succession

1580 — Began marriage negotiations with the Duke of Alençon

— Started to fund resistance to Spain in the Netherlands
50 — Failure of marriage negotiations with Alençon
— Throckmorton Plot against Elizabeth quashed
— Clashed with Parliament over the succession yet again
— Signed treaty with Dutch rebels
— Babington Plot against Elizabeth intercepted
1590 — Mary Stuart executed
— Made speech to troops at Tilbury, before the Armada
60

1600 — Made 'Golden Speech' to the House of Commons

— Announced James VI of Scotland as successor
Died 24.3.1603

1610

Elizabeth, newly crowned as Queen, in her coronation robes. This was painted in 1559.

Elizabeth I: a brief biography

How did she make history?

Elizabeth I (1533–1603) has probably had a greater impact upon English political history than any other woman. She inherited the English throne in 1558 following the death of her half-sister, **Mary Tudor**. Many contemporaries felt that she would be unable to retain the Crown, yet she survived until her natural death in 1603 and dominated the period to such an extent that it has become known as the Elizabethan age. She oversaw the establishment of a truly national Church, the defeat of Spain, the most powerful nation in the world at that time, and England's emergence as a major power. England's culture also flourished during her reign, and is epitomised by the works of William Shakespeare. Elizabeth became a national heroine; in an age dominated by men she stood out as the successful female ruler. This was also an era when all women were expected to marry, yet the 'Virgin Queen' remained unmarried throughout her reign. She exploited this, and her femininity, winning the loyalty of her subjects by claiming that she was married to the country. She stood out as a woman apart from her contemporaries and has been studied ever since. More recently, she has also been argued about, as the traditional view of her as the great Queen who could do no wrong has been challenged.

Mary Tudor (1516–58)
Mary ruled England from 1553–58. She had been declared illegitimate following Henry's marriage to Anne Boleyn but she was later restored to the succession. She succeeded to the throne upon the death of Edward VI, her half-brother. She restored Catholicism to England and rejoined England to the papacy. According to many accounts she is best remembered for burning Protestants, but more recent works have painted a much more positive picture of her achievements.

Her early life

Elizabeth I was born in 1533 at the royal palace at Greenwich. She was the only child of Henry VIII's marriage to his second wife, Anne Boleyn, but his second daughter, as his first wife, Catherine of Aragon, had already produced Mary. At that time, Henry was unable to get a divorce from the Catholic Church. Therefore, in order to marry Elizabeth's mother and obtain a male heir, Henry had broken from Rome and had begun the process known as **the English Reformation**. It was therefore a great disappointment when another daughter was born. As a result, Henry soon cast Elizabeth's mother aside and had her executed in 1536. Elizabeth, meanwhile, was declared illegitimate and lost her place in the succession.

The English Reformation: a term used to describe the religious changes that took place between 1529 and 1603 (at a legal level the religious changes were largely completed by 1559, but it was not until the 1580s that many parishes, particularly in the north-west, became Protestant).

Edward VI (1537–53)
The son of Henry VIII and Jane Seymour. He ruled England as Edward VI from 1547–53. He was a devout Protestant who succeeded to the throne upon his father's death. Recent work has shown that, although still young, he greatly influenced the religious direction of the country and helped to take it in a very Protestant direction. He was so concerned about religion that he was involved in a plot to stop his Catholic half-sister, Mary, from succeeding to the throne after his death.

The birth of **Edward** made it even more unlikely that Elizabeth would succeed to the throne so she was not brought up with a future as Queen in mind. However, this did not mean that her education suffered. Elizabeth had inherited considerable intellectual ability from her parents and was tutored by Roger Ascham and William Grindal. She mastered Latin, so that by her early teens she could read, write and speak it. By that time she was also proficient in French, Italian and Greek.

With Henry's marriage to his last wife, Catherine Parr, the situation changed for Elizabeth. Catherine helped to establish good relations once more between Henry and his daughter and a special relationship developed between Elizabeth and her stepmother. In 1544 both Mary and Elizabeth were formally restored to their places in the royal succession. Elizabeth returned to court, where she served the Queen. It was this that exposed her to the reformed religion of Protestantism. Elizabeth became an enthusiast for the new religion and demonstrated this in a New Year gift to Catherine in 1545, when she was aged 12. Elizabeth had translated a French religious poem for her, showing not only that she was able to summarise a key Protestant doctrine, that of **Justification by Faith**, but also that she had considerable linguistic skills.

Justification by Faith: the belief that, instead of good works getting you to heaven (as Catholics believed), faith alone would be enough.

The mid-Tudor crisis and survival

The death of Henry VIII, in 1547, affected Elizabeth and her position. We are told that she had 'gloried' in her father, despite her earlier treatment, but with the accession of Edward she was now second in line to the throne and a figure of far greater importance. It became important for her to protect herself, particularly from the unsuitable advances of Thomas Seymour. The illness and subsequent death of Edward in 1553 changed Elizabeth's position once again. Due to prompting from either Edward or the Duke of Northumberland, the succession was changed and both Mary and Elizabeth were excluded in favour of Lady Jane Grey.

Philip II (1527–98)
The husband of Mary Tudor and ruler of Spain and the Netherlands, he had a reputation for being a devout Catholic. It was Philip who sent the Armada against England. However, upon Elizabeth's accession to the throne, he put himself forward as a candidate for her hand in marriage.

However, this change in the succession was short-lived and Mary ascended the throne nine days after Jane had been proclaimed Queen. Although this brought Elizabeth back into the succession, her position was difficult. Mary was a devout Catholic and was determined to restore England to Rome, following the break from its authority under Henry, which had been maintained during Edward's reign. Elizabeth, as a Protestant, was a potential figurehead for any plot to remove Mary. Within months of Mary's accession, Thomas Wyatt led a rebellion to prevent Mary's marriage to **Philip II** of Spain and to replace her with Elizabeth. As the beneficiary of such a plot, Elizabeth was implicated and arrested. She was taken to the Tower and for days her life was in danger. However, no evidence to convict her could be found and she was released and placed under house arrest. This incident served to show Elizabeth how precarious her position was and she took care to keep her religious beliefs to herself. However, when Mary – on her deathbed – tried to persuade Elizabeth to promise to keep England Catholic, Elizabeth refused.

The early years as Queen

French influence in Scotland: France and Scotland were allied through the Auld Alliance, which dates back to the Middle Ages, but this had been strengthened by the marriage of James V to Mary of Guise. French influence further increased when James died and Mary was left to act as regent for her infant daughter, Mary Queen of Scots.

When she became Queen in November 1558, Elizabeth faced a number of challenges. England was threatened by invasion from France, the Catholic Church did not acknowledge her legitimacy and there were many domestic economic problems. Elizabeth was able to resolve some of these issues in the first decade of her rule and in 1559 a religious settlement was agreed (see p. 32). However, in the same year, foreign relations became more complicated as France and Spain made peace and threatened England. Despite this, Elizabeth managed to limit **French influence in Scotland** and oversaw the establishment of the Protestant Church there in 1560. Her relationship with Parliament was not always cordial because the questions of marriage and the succession kept being raised, issues that were to dominate the whole reign. Elizabeth's refusal to name an heir or commit herself resulted in heated debates and finally she forbade Parliament from discussing the issue.

Understanding Elizabeth I

- **A well-educated and intelligent woman**, who was highly literate and able to deal directly with foreign ambassadors.

- **A dominant monarch**, who was willing to assert her prerogative. She said, 'I will have one mistress and no master'.

- **A skilful propagandist**, who was aware that she needed to create the right image, she was partially responsible for the creation of a Golden Age and the cult of Gloriana, which made her the focus of plays, poems and paintings.

- **Married to her people**: it is likely that she intended to remain single from the outset and she exploited the relationship she developed with the nation.

- **A woman with a cautious and calculating nature**, which resulted from her childhood and the events of Mary Tudor's reign.

- **Believed in supporting legitimate rulers and not aiding rebels** because she feared that other rulers might aid rebels to remove her.

- **A religiously pragmatic woman**, who probably had Protestant sympathies from her childhood, but she was not a fanatic and was more concerned with outward conformity and political loyalty.

- **Loyal** to those who served her well, unlike her father, Henry VIII.

- **An excellent speaker**, who was able to persuade and inspire at crucial moments, such as at Tilbury before the Armada and in her 'Golden Speech'.

- **Refused to be bullied**, and dominated decision-making, like her father had done before her.

- **A thrifty and economical leader**, who realised that England lacked the resources of a great power and was always looking for new ways of making and saving money.

> '*Queen Elizabeth ... owing to her courage and to her great power of mind ... declines to rely on anyone save herself, although she is most gracious to all.*'
> Michel Soriano, Spanish Ambassador 1561

Mary Stuart (1542–87)
The daughter of James V of Scotland, she was seen by many Catholics as the rightful ruler of England because her grandmother was Henry VII's eldest daughter. Mary was taken to France and married to Francis II, but when he died she returned to Scotland and married Lord Darnley, a descendant of Henry VIII. Darnley was murdered by her lover, whom she then married. This led to a rebellion in Scotland and forced Mary to flee to England. She was implicated in the rebellion of the Northern Earls and other plots to remove Elizabeth. Finally she became too great a danger to Elizabeth and was executed in 1587.

Plots and invasion

The situation was made worse for Elizabeth in 1568 when **Mary Stuart** (also known as Mary Queen of Scots) fled to England. She was seen by Catholics as the rightful ruler and became the focal point for plots and conspiracies over the next 19 years. It was her arrival that sparked the only serious uprising that Elizabeth was to face, the **Northern Earls' Revolt** in 1569. However, its failure to gain widespread support suggested that the religious divide within the country was gradually being healed.

At the same time, relations with Spain were deteriorating. In 1567 England had given aid to the Netherlands in its struggle against Spain, while in 1568 Sir Francis Drake and Sir John Hawkins had begun to attack Spanish lands and had seized Spanish treasure ships. In part to counter the developing Spanish threat, Elizabeth began marriage negotiations with the French Duke of Anjou in 1570. It appeared that she would marry as she seemed to have fallen in love, but criticism of the match led her to give up her plans.

Although the Catholic threat appeared to have diminished, conspiracies continued. In 1571 the **Ridolfi Plot** was discovered. Then, from 1574, **seminary priests from Douai** began to arrive in England to spearhead a mission to Catholic families. Parliament responded by fining Catholics who did not attend the Church of England and declaring the priests guilty of treason. However, the religious question was complicated further by the growth of Puritanism. The Puritans had already tried to bring about reform through the Protestant Church, but in the 1570s they redirected their efforts towards Parliament. They began by attacking the Prayer Book in 1571 and followed this with attempts to change the rites and ceremonies in 1572. The government reacted by preventing supporters of the measures from attending Parliament and suspending some of the Puritan preachers. Finally Elizabeth

Northern Earls' Revolt: revolt in 1569 in the north of England led by the Earls of Northumberland and Westmorland. There is debate among historians about the causes, but an attempt to restore Catholicism is certainly a factor.

Ridolfi Plot: a plot by English Catholics in 1571 who intended to rebel and be supported by Spanish troops from the Netherlands. It aimed to depose Elizabeth and replace her with Mary Stuart.

Seminary priests from Douai: priests who had been trained at a special college (seminary) in Douai, France. In this context the term is usually associated with Catholic priests who were trained overseas and then came to England from 1574 onwards to minister to Catholic families.

Throckmorton Plot: this plot had the same aim as the Ridolfi Plot – to replace Elizabeth with Mary. It lasted from 1581 to 1584.

Babington Plot: in 1586, acting as a go-between for the Spanish, Babington planned to murder Elizabeth and free Mary Stuart from house arrest using Spanish troops. The correspondence between Babington and Mary was intercepted and used to persuade Elizabeth to execute Mary.

Spanish Armada: the most famous attempt by the Spanish in 1588 to launch a sea-borne invasion of England, which they did by using Spanish troops from the Netherlands. Its defeat greatly enhanced Elizabeth's position.

intervened to prevent Parliament discussing religious issues unless her bishops had given permission.

The 1580s saw an increase in problems with Catholicism and the threat from Spain. The danger posed by the Catholic Mary Stuart also appeared to be increasing with the **Throckmorton Plot** of 1583 and the **Babington Plot** of 1586. Meanwhile, Protestantism was under threat in Europe. The leader of the Dutch rebels, William of Orange, was assassinated in 1584, which forced Elizabeth to pledge to help the Dutch in their fight against Spain. This drew England and Spain into conflict and Philip II of Spain began to plan an invasion, of England. Faced with plots and the possibility of invasion, Elizabeth agreed to the execution of Mary Stuart in 1587. Elizabeth's greatest test came in 1588 when the **Spanish Armada** threatened English security. However, its scattering by English ships off the coast of Calais and its defeat at Gravelines the next day guaranteed not only English safety, but also did much to create the image of Elizabeth and England as chosen by God. The 'Protestant' wind which scattered many Spanish ships as they tried to return home was seen as God's verdict, a great boost for Elizabeth and her people.

Woodcut from 1575, showing Elizabeth at a deer hunt. As a keen devotee of the sport, she hunted regularly until she was 67 years old.

The last years

Subsidies: parliamentary grants to the sovereign for state needs.

Monopolies: sole rights in the production or sale of certain items, giving the owner complete control.

Oxfordshire rising: an attempted rising in 1596, caused by economic hardships, that failed to gain support. Despite its failure, the leaders were executed as a sign of government power and a warning to others.

Poor Law legislation: under Elizabeth, a more complex system of providing help for the poor was established. An act of 1572 made donations compulsory for the deserving poor. In the 1590s, when unemployment was a major issue, the government made a major effort to support this group as well.

Essex Rebellion: Essex wanted to increase military action against Spain, but had been unable to win support for this. At the same time he was unable to gain seats on the Privy Council or positions at court for his supporters. Instead it was the peace party, led by Burghley and Cecil, who dominated the key positions. By 1601 he was nearly bankrupt due to his failure to gain the position in the Court of Wards. He attempted to seize London, but gained little support and was easily defeated.

Unfortunately, the last decade of Elizabeth's rule did not see her build upon this success. The 1590s were a period of disappointment for many Elizabethans as the regime faltered. One success of the regime was that, with the decline of the Catholic threat, many people joined the Church of England, recognising that it was there to stay. However, after the defeat of Puritanism, some chose to leave the established Church and form their own separatist Churches. This sowed the seeds for the problems of the mid-17th century and meant that the Queen still faced many challenges despite her previous triumphs. War with Spain recurred and Elizabeth was unable to gain a decisive victory. As a result, England's finances came under great strain and Parliament would not grant the **subsidies** that were needed. Parliament also used the opportunity to attack Elizabeth's granting of **monopolies** as they raised consumer prices, which forced her to act in 1601 by cancelling some and suspending others. This preserved her prerogative of granting them, but it had forced her to concede Parliament's demands. Public discontent was made worse by the poor economic situation. A run of bad harvests had forced food prices up and even resulted in some dying from starvation. However, the fact that there was only one rebellion in the 1590s, the unsuccessful **Oxfordshire rising** of 1596, was a result of increasing government power and the success of **Poor Law legislation**.

As Elizabeth's reign entered a new century, the euphoria of her earlier years had gone. Many were disillusioned with the regime and saw it as weak and vulnerable to attack. However, the one attack it did face, the **Essex Rebellion** of 1601, was easily defeated, suggesting that despite its difficulties the regime was relatively secure. The failure of the rebellion is evidence that the Queen had not lost her grip on affairs and that the struggle between Essex and Cecil for domination at court had not allowed the country to become destabilised. When Elizabeth finally died on 24 March 1603, aged nearly 70, the succession passed peacefully to James VI of Scotland. Elizabeth had ruled England for 45 years. As England slid into civil war in the mid-17th century her achievements seemed great. This view was echoed in 1952, when Elizabeth II was crowned, and people spoke of a 'new Elizabethan age'. However, more recent historical studies have called many of Elizabeth I's achievements into question. In an age when we have become accustomed to 'political spin', Elizabeth's achievements warrant careful scrutiny before we accept the image of 'Good Queen Bess' or 'Gloriana'.

1

How consistent was Elizabeth's foreign policy?

What were its aims?

Did its direction change?

How successful was it?

Framework of events

1559	Treaty of Cateau-Cambresis. England loses Calais for eight years
1560	English army sent to Scotland. Treaty of Edinburgh. French forces withdrawn from Scotland. New Protestant government is set up
1562	Treaty of Hampton Court with French Huguenots
1564	Treaty of Troyes. England ends hostilities with France; permanent loss of Calais is confirmed
1566	Outbreak of the Dutch Revolt
1568	England seizes Spanish bullion
1572	Treaty of Blois, England and France sign defensive alliance against Spain
1581	Elizabeth starts to fund the Dutch rebels
1584	Treaty of Joinville between Catholic League and Spain
1585	Treaty of Nonsuch. Elizabeth sends 7000 troops to join the Dutch rebels in the Netherlands
1589	English troops sent to Normandy
	Spanish troops invade Brittany
1596	Alliance with Netherlands and France against Spain

What were the aims of Elizabeth's foreign policy?

In order to judge the consistency of Elizabeth's foreign policy it is essential to be clear about its aims. This is not an easy task and has led to divisions between historians. Charles Wilson, in *Queen Elizabeth and the Revolt of the Netherlands* (1970), argued that the Queen's policy was purely reactive and lacked any overall aim or objective. He maintained that England was a second-rate power, far weaker than France and Spain, who were the two major European powers. This meant that England could not afford to wage war for long and had

---

Landmark Study   The book that changed people's views

R.B. Wernham, *Before the Armada* (Cape, 1966)

Although this study does not cover the whole Elizabethan period, it is important in placing the developments in Elizabethan foreign policy in the context of the Tudor period. This book argues that a consistent pattern can be seen in the development of Tudor foreign policy as England moved from being a continental power to a maritime power. Although it is argued that even under Henry VII England was moving away from its continental ambitions, perhaps the key event in this transition was the loss of Calais that forced England to look away from Europe and towards the west. This influence meant that England's main concerns were expansion across the Atlantic, a defensive stance in Europe, based on control of the Channel and a determination to prevent any one power from having European hegemony. This was most clearly illustrated by Elizabeth's policy in the Netherlands where she was determined to prevent either France or Spain dominating. Wernham identified three key aims in Elizabeth's policy in the Netherlands and argues that these considerations were more important than dynastic or religious considerations. However, this interpretation has been challenged as some historians have argued that it is more obvious with hindsight than it was at the time. Others have suggested that there was no consistent policy of overseas expansion or patronage of voyages of discovery, and even the navy was not developed in a systematic fashion. Even Wernham responded to this criticism in later works where he acknowledges that the war against Spain was firstly a continental war.

---

little choice but to exploit chances as they occurred. However, in *Before the Armada* (1966), R.B. Wernham argued that Elizabeth's foreign policy aims and objectives were very clear, although she was not free to follow an entirely independent foreign policy because she was restricted by events in England, such as plots against her, and by the actions of foreign powers (see **Landmark Study**, above). Nevertheless foreign policy was an area of royal prerogative and, although Elizabeth sought advice from the **Privy Council**, and particularly from her Secretary of State, it was ultimately she who made the decisions. In Wallace MacCaffrey's words, in *Elizabeth I* (1993), 'the conception and initiation of policy was frequently left to the royal councillors; it became their business to devise the best possible mode of proceeding … It remained for the Queen to accept, reject or modify their proposals; there could be no question that the final decision remained a royal prerogative'. Elizabeth had her own views about foreign policy and these were important in shaping it. She wanted to avoid war because it was costly and risky. R. Sloan supported this view in *The Tudor Years* (ed. Lotherington, 1994) stating that 'she disliked the uncertainties of war and feared a lessening of her authority among those who would consider a female monarch unequal to the task of fighting one'.

Elizabeth was also unwilling to help rebels fighting against legitimate rulers in case other nations supported rebels against her in England. This would pose a real problem because there were many Catholics in England and overseas who did not view her as the legitimate ruler. Elizabeth had a strong belief in the legitimacy of **divinely appointed monarchs**, although there is little evidence that

Privy Council: a Council that advised the monarch. It usually consisted of nobles, but could include other members of the court. However, during the early part of the 16th century, an inner group had developed who met with the monarch on a regular basis.

Divinely appointed monarchs: rulers in the 16th century claimed that they were appointed by God and were his representatives on earth. This made it sinful for subjects to rebel against them and helped to strengthen the rulers' positions.

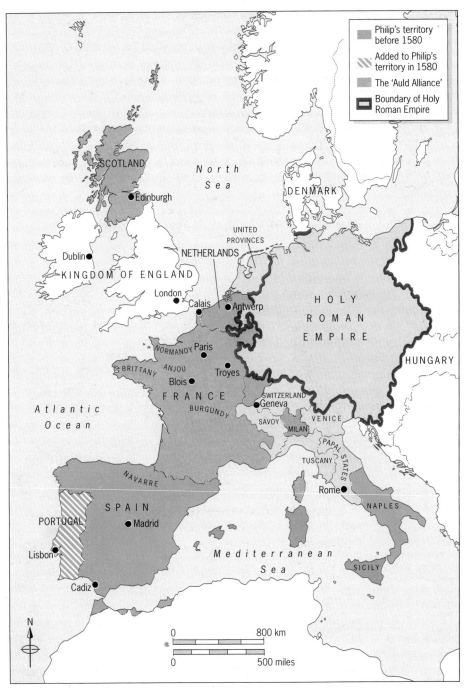

A map of Europe in the late sixteenth century, showing Philip II of Spain's possessions.

Calais: the English captured Calais in 1347. It was the last remaining English possession in France, but was seized by the French in 1558 during Mary Tudor's reign. It had been important for trade and security and its capture meant that France controlled the entire southern channel coast. Its loss was also symbolic because it represented the end of English attempts to reclaim the French Crown.

England's claim to the French throne: Elizabeth's claim to the French throne dates back to the Middle Ages when rulers of England oversaw large areas of France. During the 100 Years War (1337–1453) the English had lost all their lands except Calais, which was finally lost in 1558.

France was allied to Scotland: this was known as the 'Auld Alliance' and posed a threat to England because Scotland often attacked the northern English border when England attacked France, taking advantage of the weaker English defences.

House of Burgundy: originally a branch of the French royal family, the House of Burgundy gained lands which today are in the Netherlands. In 1477 these lands passed to the Habsburg family through marriage. England did not want France to regain the area and realised that the best defence was to be allied to the Habsburgs.

Cloth trade: unfinished cloth was taken to Antwerp to be sold.

she was motivated by religious factors. She was unwilling to act as the Protestant champion in Europe despite pressure from many of her councillors, who thought that England should fight Catholicism overseas as well as at home, and therefore she was usually reluctant to aid Protestant rebels. Unlike her Tudor predecessors, dynastic interests did not greatly influence Elizabeth's foreign policy. She would have liked to regain **Calais** but soon realised that it was lost and was unwilling to pursue **England's claim to the French throne**, recognising that it was unrealistic. She also showed a lack of dynastic concern by refusing to marry a European prince and thereby threaten England's independence, as Mary Tudor had done by marrying Philip II.

The nature of Elizabeth's foreign policy aims

It is necessary to separate general foreign policy aims that can be applied to any government at any time in history from more specific aims and objectives that applied solely to the Elizabethan period. If we were to examine general aims then it is clear that they would be to prevent the country from being invaded and from being controlled by a foreign power. However, it would be of limited value to judge policy against those simple criteria. Some specific aims can be identified:

● To assert the independence of England from France and Spain.

● To secure England's northern border. **France was allied to Scotland** and it was felt that the French would try to exploit England's poor relations with Scotland. This was a particular problem for Elizabeth at the start of her reign because Mary Stuart was married to Francis, the heir to the French throne, and therefore Franco-Scottish relations were much closer.

● To limit the power of France. France was seen as England's natural enemy and therefore it was believed that the best way to protect England was to have an alliance with the **House of Burgundy**.

● To protect the English **cloth trade** with the Netherlands. If France gained power over the Dutch coast it would control an area that could be used as a base from which to invade England. The House of Burgundy owned land in the Netherlands, which, given the French danger, was another reason for making an alliance with them. Elizabeth knew that the cloth trade was vital for ensuring social stability in England because of the numbers it employed. It also provided

Ancient liberties: the rights that the Netherlands had previously held that gave it some measure of independence. Philip was trying to reduce these and make the government of the Netherlands more centralised under Spanish authority. This was a cause of the Dutch Revolt (1566).

her with much of her income. D.M. Palliser, in *The Age of Elizabeth* (1992), has shown that cloth accounted for 78 per cent of all English exports, while wool and textiles of all kinds accounted for over 90 per cent.

● To make sure that the Channel coastline, the most likely starting point for any invasion of England, was not under the control of one power. This meant ensuring that the Netherlands retained their **ancient liberties.**

Was there a change of direction in foreign policy?

At first sight it seems obvious that Elizabeth's foreign policy lacked consistency. Her reign began with England at war with France and allied to Spain. It ended with England at war with Spain and allied to France. The threat from Scotland, which had been a major concern for previous Tudor rulers, had gone and the Scottish King, James VI, even succeeded Elizabeth as ruler of England. At the same time, England made the first tentative steps from being a second-rate power to a European and **imperial force.** Perhaps the only element of obvious consistency was the lack of money and resources available to her that informed Elizabeth's foreign policy decisions throughout her reign.

Imperial force: by the end of the 16th century, England had started to lay the foundations for an overseas empire as settlements developed in the Americas.

Guise: the most powerful Catholic noble family in France. Mary of Guise had married James V of Scotland and was the mother of Mary Stuart. She was the regent in Scotland after her husband's death.

Regent: a person appointed to administer a state because the monarch is a minor or is absent or unfit to rule.

Protestant rebellion: in Scotland the Protestant nobility, tired of rule by the foreign and Catholic Mary of Guise, started a rebellion and deposed her. By 1560 they had been successful and France withdrew from Scotland. A Council establishing Protestantism was then set up.

Relations with France and Scotland

The first issue to be resolved was the Franco-Spanish war, in which England was involved as a Spanish ally. This was settled in 1559 by the Treaty of Cateau-Cambresis between France and Spain. Under its terms England lost Calais for eight years, although in reality it was never returned. However, the ending of the war did not mean that England became friends with France. A major obstacle in the way of friendship was the 'Auld Alliance' between France and Scotland. The situation was compounded in 1559 when the French King died and Francis, Mary Stuart's husband, became King of France. French influence in Scotland was now at its height because Mary of Guise, part of the **Guise** family that controlled Francis, was the **regent** in Scotland. French troops were stationed outside Edinburgh and an extra force was about to be sent. To further complicate the issue, a **Protestant rebellion** had broken out in Scotland. Although Elizabeth disliked aiding rebels against lawful rulers, she acted decisively and sent financial help to them. At the end of the year she sent an English fleet to stop the French sending

French Wars of Religion: the wars in France from 1562–98, caused, in part, by the spread of Calvinism and by powerful nobles who saw the chance to exploit royal weakness after the death of Henry II. The situation was made worse because the two most powerful families, the Guises and the Bourbons, were divided by religion. These wars divided France and largely kept her out of European affairs for the last part of the 16th century.

Huguenots: the name given to French Calvinists.

Duke of Anjou (1551–89)
He was the second son of Catherine de Medici (the regent of France). He was involved in marriage negotiations with Elizabeth in 1569, and became Henry III of France in 1574.

further forces and finally, in 1560, she signed a treaty with the Scottish Protestants and sent them military aid.

These actions appear to contradict Elizabeth's foreign policy objectives of maintaining peace and refusing to aid rebels trying to depose lawful rulers. However, it was vital for national security that the power of the Guise family in Scotland was reduced. Elizabeth lacked the resources for a full-scale war against France, but saw in Scotland an opportunity to reduce French influence and secure England's northern border. It is unlikely that she helped the Protestants for religious reasons, despite pressure from her Council. According to Susan Doran, in *England and Europe 1485–1603* (1986), Elizabeth was reluctant to give financial or military aid to the Protestant party in Scotland and offered support only when further French intervention appeared likely. Her policy was consistent since she was continuing a Tudor principle of securing England's borders. However, it can be argued that the means of achieving security had changed and that Elizabeth understood the need to aid Scottish Protestant forces to prevent the French from recovering influence in Scotland.

The Scottish question had raised the issue of England's relations with its traditional enemy, France. This became more complicated in 1562 with the outbreak of the **French Wars of Religion**. Elizabeth was under pressure from some of her councillors to aid the **Huguenots**, who were doing badly in the struggle, and thus further national security by weakening France. Elizabeth's decision to intervene on the side of the Huguenots could be regarded as inconsistent because they were fighting a lawful ruler. However, Doran argues that 'the possible recovery of Calais attracted her to the Huguenot cause'. This suggests that dynastic gains featured in Elizabeth's concerns, but if that is true, the defeat suffered in France by the Huguenots soon encouraged her to abandon the idea.

Relations with France during Elizabeth's reign seem erratic at first sight. England was at war with France in 1559, drove the French out of Scotland in 1560 and aided the Huguenots in the early 1560s. This was followed by peace in 1564, an alliance in 1572 and marriage negotiations in 1569 with the **Duke of Anjou** and in 1572 with the **Duke of Alençon**. In order to understand

Duke of Alençon (1554–84) He was the youngest son of Catherine de Medici and took the Duke of Anjou's	title when he became King Henry III. Elizabeth was serious in her desire to marry him and negotiations lasted, on and off, from	1572 to 1584. He also led French armies into the Netherlands to help the Dutch in their fight against Spain.

Heretical: holding a religious opinion that does not agree with the generally accepted belief. In the 16th century Catholics viewed Protestants as heretics.

Catholic League: an organisation formed in France by the leading Catholic families, with Spanish aid, to prevent the Protestant Henry of Navarre from taking the throne.

Henry of Navarre (1553–1610)
The nearest male relative to Henry III, but he was Protestant. The Guise family wanted to exclude him from the succession. This re-started the fighting in the French Wars of Religion. Henry III was assassinated in 1589, but he had recognised Henry as heir, which intensified the civil war. Elizabeth provided financial aid for Henry to fight the Catholic League. In 1593, he announced his conversion to Catholicism. This brought about a truce with the Catholic League and an agreement that all foreign troops should leave France. In 1595 he declared war on Spain.

Channel ports: ports in France and the Netherlands that could be used for an invasion of England.

Counter-Reformation: the Catholic response to the Protestant Reformation. One of its aims was to regain lands lost to Protestantism.

England's changing relations with France, it is necessary to see them in the context of developments in the Netherlands. The outbreak of disturbances in the Netherlands and the large Spanish army there forced Elizabeth to improve relations with France. It was vital for English security that Spain and France did not become allied, thus leaving England isolated. The best way of ensuring this was for England to ally with France. It was for this reason that England signed the Treaty of Blois with France in 1572, which committed the two countries to helping each other if they were attacked by Spain. Elizabeth's policy towards France was shaped by her reluctance to aid rebels, this time the Dutch, and by her lack of the financial and military resources necessary to wage a full-scale war against the Spanish. This partially explains her decision to pursue marriage negotiations with the Duke of Alençon since it would stop France joining Spain. When the plans failed she offered aid to Anjou to fight the Spanish in the Netherlands, but he was defeated in 1583 at Antwerp. Sloan concludes that this policy towards France helped Elizabeth to achieve her aims because 'friendship with France would force Philip to compete for her favour. It might help to restrain French ambition in the Netherlands. Finally, it would stave off the possibility that the two great Catholic powers would unite against a **heretical** England'.

A major problem arose for Elizabeth in 1584 with the development of the **Catholic League** in France and its alliance with Spain. This seriously threatened English security because a future crusade against England appeared likely. In order to protect national security Elizabeth supported the Huguenot leader **Henry of Navarre** in his struggle against the French Crown. Henry finally became King in 1589 and Elizabeth continued to support him with military aid, sending troops in 1589 and 1591 and maintaining a military force in Brittany in order to prevent the Spanish from gaining control of the **Channel ports**.

Elizabeth's reign after the Treaty of Troyes in 1564 was dominated by concerns about national security. She was determined to keep France and Spain apart and to stop them becoming allies in a **Counter-Reformation** crusade against England, particularly after the Treaty of Joinville, which heightened the risk of a Spanish attack on England. Elizabeth wanted to use France against Spain in the Netherlands and to prevent both Spain and the Catholic League from controlling the Channel ports. Wernham argues that she was unwilling to see French power grow in the Netherlands and, because she did not trust the French, she thought that the best policy was to check them by co-operating with them in various ways. Relations between the two countries changed and improved during the period mainly because Spain became the common enemy.

Relations with Spain and the Netherlands

At the centre of Elizabethan foreign policy were relations with Spain and the Netherlands. The two countries were inextricably linked because the Netherlands was part of the Spanish Empire and ruled by Philip II. The Netherlands was commercially essential for the cloth trade and strategically vital for English security because it was seen as the best place from which to launch an invasion of England. Wernham argues that Elizabeth had three clear aims in the Netherlands:

Charles V (1500–58)
The father of Philip II and ruler of Spain and the Netherlands from 1516–56, Charles V was also Holy Roman Emperor from 1519–56, which gave him control over large areas of land in what is now Germany.

- to remove the Spanish army

- to prevent France from gaining control and thereby threatening English security by controlling all the Channel ports

- to return the Netherlands to self-government, as it had been under **Charles V**

Thus Elizabeth's aim throughout the period was to prevent Spain and France from gaining control of the area. Philip therefore posed a great threat to Elizabeth in his attempts to gain more direct control over the Netherlands. Wernham is right when he argues that 'she wanted the Netherlands, though restored to their ancient liberties, to remain Spanish so that they would not become French'. The outbreak of the **Dutch Revolt** in 1566 made the area even more important. It was a battleground between Protestantism and Catholicism, but once again, despite pressure from some of her councillors, Elizabeth chose to intervene for strategic, rather than religious, reasons.

Dutch Revolt: a revolt that broke out in the Spanish Netherlands. There were many causes, including Philip's attempt to increase his control, but the issue was further complicated by religious divisions. The revolt lasted into the 17th century and eventually saw the northern provinces of the Netherlands gain their independence from Spain.

Relations with Spain were friendly for at least the first decade of Elizabeth's reign. It was fortunate for Elizabeth that Philip wanted England's friendship as much as England needed Spain's. Philip proved this by his offer of marriage and his role in preventing the Pope from excommunicating Elizabeth in the early 1560s. Both countries saw France as the main danger and Elizabeth needed to maintain Spanish friendship as a balance to France. However, there were some early indications of worsening relations, particularly

Francis Drake (1540–96)
He started his maritime career in slaving expeditions, and then turned to attacking the Spanish silver fleet as it sailed from South America to Spain. In 1577, he circumnavigated the world and was knighted. This saw him move from operating a privateer into royal service and the post of the Queen's Admiral. He attacked the Spanish West Indies in 1585 and led the expedition against Cadiz in 1587, destroying 24 Spanish ships. In 1588, he was involved against the Armada. He retired in 1589, but returned to action in 1595 to attack the Spanish. However, the expedition failed and Drake died of dysentery.

John Hawkins (1532–95)
He was Drake's cousin and made his name in the early Elizabethan period as a slave trader. In 1578, he was appointed comptroller of the navy and set about changing the design of ships. He was commander of the navy during the Armada and died in 1595 during Drake's final expedition.

Privateers: armed ships owned by private individuals, holding government commissions and authorised for use in war.

Genoese loan: money loaned by Italian bankers from the city of Genoa. It was being transported by sea to the Netherlands when a storm forced the ships into an English port, enabling Elizabeth to seize the money.

with the activities of **privateers**, operated by men such as **Francis Drake** and **John Hawkins**, in the West Indies and Africa. Yet it was events in the Netherlands that were to end the traditional Tudor alliance with Spain.

The major cause of the deterioration in relations was England's seizure of Spanish ships carrying a **Genoese loan** to the Netherlands in 1568. This money was intended to pay for the Spanish army present in the Netherlands to put down the Dutch Revolt. Elizabeth was concerned that a Spanish victory would free the army to launch an attack on England. Lacking the financial and military power necessary to take on the Spanish, her next best option was to disrupt Spanish efforts to quell the Dutch Revolt. By prolonging it, she could keep the Spanish soldiers busy and thereby prevent them from being used in an attack on England. The Spanish ambassador in England advised the commander of the Spanish army in the Netherlands to respond by seizing all English merchants and their goods, which brought about a standstill in trade between England and the Netherlands. Elizabeth retaliated by ordering instant reprisals on all Spanish subjects in England. According to Wilson, Elizabeth's seizure of the Genoese loan was senseless, but George Ramsay, in *The Reign of Elizabeth I* (ed. Haigh, 1984), has argued that it was the actions of the Spanish ambassador in England that wrecked the old Anglo-Spanish alliance and prevented a settlement of the issue.

Although attempts were made during the 1570s to improve relations with Spain, this period saw a turning point in Anglo-Spanish relations. Spain became increasingly involved in the Netherlands and Elizabeth was dragged into the conflict, and

William of Orange (1533–84)
A member of the Dutch nobility, he was the Prince of Orange and governor of three provinces. He was brought up a Lutheran, but converted to Catholicism. He resigned all his offices and fled the country when Philip despatched a military force to the Netherlands. As a result, he lost all his possessions, and in 1568 launched an invasion to regain them that failed. He returned in 1572 and put himself at the head of the rebels, converting to Calvinism in 1573. He was assassinated in 1584.

eventually into war against Spain, because of her concern over Spanish control of the Netherlands and the associated threat to national security. Spain began to win back territory, causing Elizabeth to mediate to have the Spanish army removed and the Netherlands restored to self-government. This supports Sloan's argument that Elizabeth did not seek the outright defeat of Spain, but favoured a return to the situation as it had been under Charles V. When attempts at negotiation failed she tried to use foreign troops to help the rebels, but this failed in 1578 and 1581. When the leader of the Dutch rebels, **William of Orange**, was assassinated in 1584, Elizabeth was forced into military action because it looked like the rebels would be defeated and Spain would increase its control over the whole area. In the same year, Spain had signed an alliance with the Catholic League and it seemed that, once the rebels were crushed in the Netherlands, Spain and France would be free to launch a crusade against England.

When Elizabeth signed the Treaty of Nonsuch in 1585, she appeared to be abandoning her principles of not supporting a rebel force against a lawful monarch and of avoiding war. However, it can be argued that she was making a last desperate bid to keep England independent. Philip had become involved in many of the Catholic plots within England to remove Elizabeth and in 1580 he had become King of Portugal, which gave him a navy large enough to challenge England.

Most historians agree that the decision to go to war with Spain in 1585 was correct. The war was fought in a number of areas – the Netherlands, Ireland and the New World – but its most famous battle was the Armada of 1588. There were very few occasions when English and Spanish troops actually clashed because, aware of the weakness of English forces, Elizabeth used her navy to attack the vulnerable parts of the Spanish Empire. Although the decision to send the Armada was Philip's, it can be argued that Elizabeth's actions brought England to the brink of invasion. Under the Treaty of Nonsuch she had sent **Robert Dudley, Earl of Leicester**

Robert Dudley, Earl of Leicester (1532–88)
He was a son of the Duke of Northumberland who had ruled during the reign of Edward VI. He had been in the Tower because of his part in his father's plot to replace Mary Tudor with Lady Jane Grey. When Elizabeth became Queen, he was made Master of the Horse. There were rumours of a close romantic attachment between Elizabeth and Dudley, despite his marriage, which caused distrust among other councillors. He wanted England to champion Protestantism on the continent. In 1562, he joined the council and clashed frequently with Cecil. He was created Lord Leicester in 1564 and died in 1588.

to the Netherlands to aid the rebels, but had given him insufficient forces, which were unable to halt the Spanish advance. Leicester had worsened relations with Spain by taking the title of Governor General, implying that Elizabeth aimed to replace Spanish sovereignty over the Netherlands with English rule. Moreover, Drake's attacks on **Spanish silver fleets** and his sacking of **San Domingo and Cartagena** added to the tensions. This was compounded by his daring attack on **Cadiz** in 1587.

Although the Armada was defeated, its importance has been exaggerated. Christopher Haigh has argued in *Elizabeth I* (1988) that even after the Armada 'there was still a successful army in the Netherlands, still Spanish support for French Catholics against the Huguenots, and still a risk of Spanish invasion'. Nevertheless, Elizabeth had prevented invasion on this occasion and the navy had shown that it could protect England, even if it could not win the war. Philip launched other attacks in 1596 and 1597, which also failed. When Spanish troops did make a successful landing, in Ireland in 1601, they were swiftly massacred. Elizabeth had been successful in her main objective of preserving national security.

In conclusion, it is probably fair to say that Elizabeth's objectives changed during her reign and that this made her policy appear inconsistent. It had become apparent that France was not England's natural enemy; Spain represented the greatest threat to England because of its sovereignty over the Netherlands and this is reflected in the deterioration of relations with Spain and improved relations with France. However, Elizabeth's consistent aim was to ensure the independence of the Netherlands.

Spanish silver fleets: ships bringing gold and silver from the Spanish New World to Spain. They were a vital source of revenue for the Spanish.

San Domingo and Cartagena: settlements in the Spanish New World.

Cadiz: a major Spanish port where the Armada assembled. By destroying the ships, England delayed the Armada.

How successful was Elizabeth's foreign policy?

Although some historians, such as John Neale in *Queen Elizabeth I* (1934) and A.L. Rowse in *The England of Elizabeth* (1950), have seen Elizabeth's reign as a time of greatness during which England emerged as the leading power in Western Europe, others have adopted a more negative view. Paul Crowson took such a view in *Tudor Foreign Policy* (1973), arguing that the 45 years of her reign were a time of pessimism, insecurity and national danger. Wilson supported this interpretation, particularly with reference to events in the Netherlands, arguing that Elizabeth demonstrated an unreasonable fear of France, given that it was weakened by civil war. He concluded that Elizabeth's policy in the Netherlands was a failure and argued that her cautiousness in the 1570s lost her the opportunity to exploit her advantages. Wilson maintained that if

The Armada Portrait. This shows Elizabeth as 'the great Empress of the world'. She has defeated her enemies and her dress emphasises the wealth of her realm. She is looking at the fireships that had scattered the Armada. On the globe her hand rests on the Americas, where English ships have also beaten the Spanish.

Embargo: an order given by a state forbidding foreign ships to enter or any ships to leave its ports.

England had intervened in the Dutch Revolt with full-scale military help it would have ensured the creation of a friendly Protestant Dutch Republic. This would have won her much support at home because many Protestants wanted her to aid co-religionists in the struggle against Catholicism. However, this interpretation is based on the belief that Elizabeth wanted to establish a Calvinist state in the Netherlands, whereas her main concern was to maintain Spanish sovereignty in order to prevent French expansion. She also did not want to antagonise the Spanish and face an **embargo**.

Elizabeth did not want a war with the mightiest power in Europe unless it was essential, which was not the case in the 1570s. Therefore she followed alternative policies that historians such as Wernham argue were a success. He believes that if the main aims of Elizabethan foreign policy were to protect national security and prevent invasion, then it was a success. Elizabeth faced challenges to the Crown at various times from France, Spain and Scotland and, despite being less powerful, was able to defeat them. It is to her credit that, unlike France, she avoided religious conflict within England and prevented foreign powers from becoming involved in it as had happened with Spain in France, when Spanish troops helped the Catholic League in its fight against the Huguenots. Despite a lack of resources and a costly war with Spain that went on for the last 15 years of her reign, she avoided bankrupting England, although there was resentment in England at the high level of taxation.

However, it is possible that Elizabeth was fortunate and that her success owed much to circumstances beyond her control. She was lucky that the Armada failed because England lacked the military resources to defeat a full-scale land invasion. She was lucky that the Guises failed in their bid to control France and Scotland because, in alliance with Spain, they would have been a serious threat to national security. Lastly, she was lucky that Mary Stuart made so many mistakes, giving Elizabeth the opportunity to remove her without too much of an outcry.

However, her policy in Scotland was a clear success. Doran supports this view, arguing that 'the subsequent establishment of Protestantism in Scotland effectively closed that country to French influence'. This argument can be taken further because the Guise family was forced to make peace so that they could concentrate on growing problems at home, which meant that France's threat was neutralised for some years. However, Elizabeth did not see her policy in Scotland as a success because she had hoped to regain Calais through the Treaty of Edinburgh, signed in 1560. It also worried her that this supposed success would mean that she was viewed as the protector of Protestant rebels and thus the enemy of France and Spain.

Intervention in France in the early years brought less obvious advantages. In 1562 it failed because the Huguenots were defeated and made peace with the Catholics to drive England out. Then, in 1564, Calais was lost forever in the Treaty of Troyes. However, the later period of her reign saw Elizabeth achieve her aims. The French were prevented from replacing the Spanish in the Netherlands and the Catholic League was unable to join with the Spanish to launch a crusade against England. Henry of Navarre secured the French throne and, although he became Catholic, realised that Spain, rather than England, was France's enemy. As a result England was not threatened by a Franco-Spanish challenge and it was therefore much easier for England to maintain its independence.

It can be argued that Elizabeth's policy towards Spain was a failure since England was faced with a protracted war that could not be won. However, as Doran argues, Elizabeth ultimately achieved her aims. Spain was not defeated, but it was distracted by events in the Netherlands and prevented from launching an invasion until 1588. The southern provinces of the Netherlands were restored to Spain, but under terms of semi-independence, as they had been under Charles V. The northern provinces gained full independence, which meant that the French were kept out and that the area could not be used to launch an invasion of England. In war and peace Elizabeth sought national security; she had achieved it.

How consistent was Elizabeth's foreign policy?

1. Read the following extract and answer the question.

'To dignify the dealings of Elizabeth Tudor and her continental neighbours with the title 'foreign policy' perhaps suggests more than her hesitant groping could substantiate. The old-fashioned principles lost their relevance in little more than a decade. With the collapse of the Antwerp cloth market 1569–73, the English cloth trade was released from its traditional dependence upon the House of Burgundy. Left to fend for herself, she struck up an entente with the Valois princes of France and reluctantly took up the cudgels on behalf of the rebels of the Netherlands, thereby preserving north-west Europe from complete domination by her enemies.'

(adapted from G.R. Ramsay, 'The Foreign Policy of Elizabeth I', in *The Reign of Elizabeth I*, ed. Haigh, Macmillan, 1984, p. 167)

How far does Ramsay successfully explain the nature and changes in English foreign policy under Elizabeth I?

2. How far did Elizabeth achieve her aims in foreign policy?

2

Who presented Elizabeth with the greater threat: Catholics or Puritans?

> ### How serious was the Catholic threat?

> ### How serious was the Puritan threat?

Framework of events

1559	Acts of Supremacy and Uniformity
	Royal Injunctions set out religious beliefs
1563	Thirty Nine Articles
1566	Parker's Advertisements and the Vestments controversy
1568	Mary Stuart flees to England
1569	Northern Rebellion
1570	Pope Pius V issues Papal Bull *'Regnans in Excelsis'*
1574	First missionary priests from Douai arrive in England
1576	Archbishop Grindal refuses to suppress prophesyings
1580	First Jesuits arrive in England
1583	Whitgift becomes Archbishop of Canterbury upon death of Grindal
1587	Cope's Bill and Book
	Execution of Mary Stuart
1588	Defeat of the Armada
1589	Marprelate Tracts published
1593	Act against Seditious Sectaries
1598	Appointment of the first Archpriest

How serious was the Catholic threat?

Historians have found it very difficult to agree on the threat presented by Catholicism to the stability of England under Elizabeth. Firstly it is necessary to distinguish between the threat from Catholics in England and those abroad, particularly Spain. Any assessment is frequently determined by views about the nature and timescale of the English Reformation. Alan Dickens, in his work *The English Reformation* (1964), argues that the move towards Protestantism was fast and, in a large part, driven by a popular dislike for the Catholic Church. Dickens argues that 'the majority of people cannot possibly have been ardent or even convinced Catholics'. According to this interpretation, support for Catholicism was minimal by the time Elizabeth I came to the throne and, therefore, was of little threat to her. Catholicism would only become an issue when revived by the arrival of seminary priests in 1574.

This remained the traditional view until the late 1980s when it was challenged by historians such as Christopher Haigh in *The English Reformation Revised* (see **Landmark Sudy**, p. 35). He argues that Catholicism was not in persistent decline and shows how it was still strong under Elizabeth's predecessor, Mary Tudor. This interpretation suggests that Catholicism presented a serious problem for Elizabeth in the early decades of her reign, and helps to explain the very cautious policy she followed in the early years. Eammon Duffy supports this argument in his book, *The Stripping of the Altars* (1992), in which he shows that, outside London and the south-east, much of England was still Catholic until the 1580s.

The Marian legacy

According to the traditionalist interpretation represented by Dickens, Mary I's policy of trying to turn England back to Catholicism was doomed to failure. Popular anti-Catholic feeling, partly induced by the harsh policy of the burning of Protestants during Mary's reign, had ensured that England would remain a Protestant country. If this reading is correct, the Catholic menace to Elizabeth was minimal.

However, this view has been challenged by **revisionist historians**. They have shown that the triumph of Protestantism was far from guaranteed and that, just because it succeeded, it was not certain in 1558 when Elizabeth came to the throne. These historians have argued that the ease with which Mary restored Catholicism during the five years of her reign showed that it was far from dying and that there was popular support for its restoration. It will always be difficult to assess the number of Catholics and Protestants in England in 1558, but it is unlikely that Protestantism had made great headway throughout the country. The nation had experienced only a few years of Protestant rule under Edward VI (1547–53) and these had been unpopular, as the number of religious rebellions that occurred during this time, such as the **Western Rebellion** of

Revisionist historians: historians who have challenged the accepted interpretation of a particular event and put forward a new explanation.

Western Rebellion: also known as the Prayer Book Rebellion. It took place in the counties of Devon and Cornwall and was largely a protest against the First Prayer Book introduced under Edward VI, which was regarded as too Protestant for many Catholics.

1549, shows. This was then followed by five years of Catholic rule by Mary, which would suggest that Catholicism was still a major force when Elizabeth came to the throne.

The challenge to the religious settlement of 1559

The revisionist view is supported by the problems Elizabeth faced in trying to achieve a religious settlement at the start of her reign (see p. 32). Although traditional accounts have argued that she was forced into a more radical settlement than she wanted, because of the strength of Protestant feeling, this view is now largely discredited. It took a lot of careful manipulation, as has been popularised in the film *Elizabeth* (1998), for the settlement to get through Parliament. The Act of Supremacy was passed by the House of Lords, despite wholesale opposition from the bishops, because only one layman voted against it. Meanwhile, the Act of Uniformity was only passed by the House of Lords because of the absence of the Abbot of Westminster and the imprisonment of two bishops in the Tower. This would suggest that the Catholic threat was strong and it helps to explain why Elizabeth moved cautiously in the early years of her reign.

JPs: Justices of the Peace. Their main task was to see that laws were obeyed in their area. They were appointed for every county, and under Elizabeth their numbers increased as did their powers. A small county might have had 15, while a large county might have had up to 80.

In order to enforce the settlement she was dependent upon **JPs**, local gentry and priests. However, because many of them were Catholic, the settlement was not implemented in many localities. Elizabeth had little choice but to turn a blind eye to priests who said Mass so that she could try to win over the population, rather than alienate them and provoke a possible rebellion. However, the situation could have been a lot worse for Elizabeth. Many Catholics were uncertain how to act. Some had even hidden images ready to use when the Catholic faith was restored and were waiting for the Pope to give instructions on how to act, but nothing happened. It was only the Pope's lack of early action that allowed Elizabeth to establish both herself and her Church.

Legality of Henry's marriage: the legality of the marriage was questioned because the divorce had been carried out in England and Catherine was not allowed to challenge its legality in Rome. Catholics did not accept that Henry had this right, and believed that only the Pope could oversee a divorce.

The legitimacy of Elizabeth

Elizabeth's position was further weakened by doubts about her legitimacy. In the eyes of Catholics she was illegitimate because they did not recognise the **legality of Henry's marriage** to Anne Boleyn. As a result, they regarded Mary Stuart as the legitimate heir. However, Elizabeth was fortunate because the Pope avoided taking a stand against her, perhaps hoping that she would return to the Catholic faith. She was also protected by Philip II of Spain who had hopes of marrying her. Philip also feared Mary Stuart, with her **French connections**, ruling England and threatening the Spanish

French connections: Mary's father, James V of Scotland, had married the French Mary of Guise.

The religious settlement of 1559

The process of achieving the settlement
was not easy. The Acts that constituted the
settlement were the Act of Uniformity and
the Act of Supremacy. However, these did
not deal with all areas so the Royal
Injunctions were issued.

The Act of Supremacy

- This gave Elizabeth the title 'Supreme
  Governor' of the Church of England,
  changing it from 'Supreme Head',
  which had been Henry's title. In
  practice it gave her the same powers as
  her father, but avoided controversy by
  trying to please those who saw the
  Pope as the rightful head or did not
  believe that a woman could be head of
  the Church. This appealed to both
  Catholics and extreme Protestants.
- People had to swear an oath of loyalty.
  Commissioners were sent out to
  enforce this and could prosecute those
  who refused to swear the oath. This
  allowed Elizabeth to replace Catholic
  priests and JPs with those of a more
  Protestant persuasion.
- Church organisation remained the
  same with a hierarchy of archbishops
  and bishops. This displeased many
  Puritans who wanted to see each
  congregation running its own church.

The Act of Uniformity

- Introduced the New Book of Common
  Prayer and attempted to appeal to
  everyone.
- Defined how churches should be
  decorated.
- Replaced altars with the more
  Protestant communion tables, although

Catholic decorations such as crosses
and candles could be placed on them.
- Ensured that the dress of the priests
  remained largely Catholic.

The Royal Injunctions

- Preachers had to be licensed.
  Licensing was put in place so that the
  government could curb the number of
  more radical Puritan preachers.
- Preachers had to preach at least once
  every month.
- Every church had to possess a Bible in
  English. This measure pleased
  Protestants, who wanted a Bible that
  was accessible to all, so that they could
  think for themselves rather than have
  to rely on a priest.
- Pilgrimages were banned. This was an
  attack on a Catholic practice.
- No more altars were to be destroyed.
  This would have pleased Catholics and
  disappointed Puritans.
- Wafers could still be used at
  communion, which pleased Catholics.
- The instruction forbidding kneeling at
  communion was removed, displeasing
  Puritans, who thought the practice
  suggested a 'real presence'.

It is clear that neither group would have
been completely satisfied or dissatisfied by
this settlement; it was a compromise. The
Church organisation owed much to the
Catholic model of a clear hierarchy.
However, the state control was more in
common with Protestant churches. The
religious changes were largely Protestant,
but not enough to alienate Catholics
totally. However, many Protestants did not
think the changes went far enough.

sea route to the Netherlands. This unexpected support allowed Elizabeth more time to secure her position and it went a long way to lessening the Catholic threat in the early years of her reign.

The policy of continuity

Desiderius Erasmus (c.1466–1536)
A well-known and respected European scholar. Despite being Catholic, he translated and interpreted the Bible. He attacked relics, rituals and the structure of monastic life. He had a great impact in England and inspired a group of scholars who became known as humanists. They wanted a simple religion, based on a more accurate translation of the Bible.

Crucifix: a cross with a figure of Christ on it. This was seen by many as a symbol of Catholicism.

Elizabeth was very careful to ensure, particularly in the early years, that her Church resembled the old Catholic Church in as many ways as possible, thus making it easier for many Catholics to attend services. Throughout her reign, Elizabeth was under pressure to alter the religious settlement of 1559 and make it more Protestant, but she refused to do this, realising that any such move would alienate those Catholics who were prepared to conform. She was also aware that she could not replace the existing clergy with trained Protestants because they were not available in sufficiently large numbers. It was chiefly for this reason that she followed a policy of continuity. She also realised that, if Catholics attended the new services for long enough and saw their neighbours present, they would gradually conform. They were more likely to do this if the services resembled Catholic rites in as many ways as possible.

She encouraged this through the Royal Injunctions of 1559. Although these required each parish to possess a Bible in English, which displeased Catholics, they also required a copy of **Desiderius Erasmus**' *Paraphrases*, a work by a Catholic writer. The Injunctions also required people to bow at the name of Jesus, kneel at prayer and called for the clergy to wear clerical dress. Even clerical marriage, that most Protestant of tenets, was not actively encouraged since priests who wanted to marry had to obtain the permission of their bishop and two JPs. There was controversy over the question of the **crucifix** too. Elizabeth wanted each church to retain a crucifix and to restore those that had been destroyed. This was undoubtedly a Catholic ornament and some bishops threatened to resign. Elizabeth backed down, but kept one in the Royal Chapel so that visitors would see how close to Catholicism the new service really was. With these moves, many Catholics probably saw little reason to risk open rebellion. Therefore it can be argued that the potential threat from the large number of Catholics in England at the start of Elizabeth's reign was nullified by stressing the similarities between the new and old services.

The problem of priests and local government

The policy of continuity for the shift from Catholicism to Protestantism was also advisable given the situation in the parishes and amongst local government officials. Elizabeth was forced to depend on the existing clergy until there were sufficient numbers of trained Protestants, but penalised them if they failed to follow the specified order of service. However, these penalties were not excessively harsh. A first offence brought six months' imprisonment and a fine, the second a year's imprisonment and the third life imprisonment. She did not make the same mistake as Mary and create martyrs. Elizabeth used the same approach for dealing with the laity; they were fined for non-attendance. However, it was easily possible to avoid being penalised because the levying of the fine depended upon it being reported by the churchwardens, who were often unwilling to report parishioners for absence. This policy may have allowed Catholicism to survive well into Elizabeth's reign, but it also meant that many Catholics saw no point in being involved in plots and rebellion since it would be likely to make their position worse. By a cautious policy Elizabeth allowed Catholicism to die out naturally while future generations grew up in the ritual and establishment of the Church of England. Time had probably been her greatest ally as the new order gradually became accepted.

The number of Catholics

Although it appears that the majority of the population was Catholic in 1558, numbers went into steady decline. Encouraged in part by the policies of Elizabeth, but also by the inactivity of the papacy, Catholicism in England had declined significantly by 1570. The situation for Catholics was not helped by the **Papal Bull** of 1570. By forbidding Catholics to attend English church services, the Pope made them face fines, which many could not afford to pay. They also felt forced into a choice between loyalty to their friends, neighbours and the state or to their Church; few were prepared to put the latter first.

Papal Bull: an edict issued by the papacy which all Catholics are expected to obey. The bull of 1570 called on Catholics to depose Elizabeth. This caused many problems, in particular the issue of divided loyalty.

The arrival in 1574 of seminary priests from Douai in France presented the government with a new challenge, but it may also have ensured that the survival of Catholicism would be more unlikely. The aim of these priests was not only to keep alive the faith among the Catholic population, but to convert others. The priests sought protection from Catholic gentry but the government was forced to take a harsh attitude towards both Catholics and priests. Of 438 priests who arrived, 98 were captured and put to death. However,

Landmark Study The book that changed people's views

Christopher Haigh, *The English Reformation Revised* (Cambridge University Press, 1987)

This is the classic revisionist book that went a long way to destroying the Dickens thesis. In this and other subsequent writings, Haigh has argued that Catholicism was not suffering inevitable decline. He showed that the survival of Catholicism did not depend upon the arrival of missionary priests and that arguments that supported this view were based upon evidence from the priests themselves, who were bound to stress their role. A great deal of his evidence came from regional studies, particularly of Lancashire, and this can be followed up by reading his book, *Reformation and Resistance in Tudor Lancashire* (1975). His evidence also came from the visitation records made by the Elizabethan bishops. The argument that Catholicism was not in widespread decline has also influenced our views about the progress of the Protestant Reformation and Haigh has shown convincingly that many northern areas did not become Protestant before the late 1580s.

once again Elizabeth did not make the same mistake as Mary; the priests were put to death for treason, not heresy, and therefore were not seen as martyrs by the majority of the population.

Just as importantly, recent work by historians such as Haigh (see **Landmark Study**, above) has shown that much of the priests' missionary activity was misdirected. He has argued that they concentrated most of their missionary work in the south-east of England where there were fewer Catholics. This made the task for the priests much harder and also meant that the north and west of England, where Catholicism had more support, were neglected and the faith allowed to wither. The missionary cause was further weakened by divisions within the movement between the **Jesuits**

Jesuits: a religious order founded in 1534 known for their dedicated service to the Pope. They were seen as arch-enemies of anti-Catholic beliefs and were very important in the resistance against Protestantism throughout Europe.

A Jesuit being tortured. The Jesuits were seen by the government as a major threat and were often tortured for confessions that they were involved in plots to overthrow Elizabeth. Elizabeth wanted to have them executed for political, not religious, reasons and therefore wanted them to admit they were involved in plots to remove her.

and the priests from Douai. There were already difficulties between the two groups: the Jesuits rejected any form of compromise with the Elizabethan government, whilst the priests from Douai stressed the political loyalty of English Catholics. The tensions between the two groups came to a head in 1598 with the **Archpriest controversy**. The situation had been further weakened by the deaths, due to old age, of many priests in the 1590s. Catholicism could not survive without priests and therefore in counties such as Yorkshire, where Catholicism had been strong, it faded.

Archpriest controversy: it was decided to appoint a head priest to supervise the Catholic Church in England. The appointment of a Jesuit had been opposed in England and when the case was finally taken to Rome, the decision to prevent representatives from England attending added to the outrage of many English Catholics.

Plots and rebellion

Elizabeth did not face a Catholic rebellion until 1569, over ten years after she came to the throne. Some historians even argue that the rebellion of the Northern Earls (see p. 12) was not caused by religious factors, but was due to the powers of central government in London increasing at the expense of the traditional northern families of Northumberland and Westmorland. The rebellion failed to appeal to the masses, with only 5000 supporters compared to the 40 000 who had supported the **Pilgrimage of Grace** in 1536. This suggests that most regarded loyalty to the Queen as more important than loyalty to their religion. The rebellion's failure to gather numbers on its way southwards suggests that the Reformation had certainly taken hold in the south and midlands at least.

Pilgrimage of Grace: this rebellion was thought by many historians to have been caused by Henry VIII closing the monasteries. At its height, some 40 000 rebels were involved. They took the royal castle at Pontefract and Henry was unable to raise a large enough army to defeat them. He was therefore forced to negotiate.

However, it would be unwise to dismiss the threat the rebellion posed. The rebels celebrated the Mass in Durham Cathedral and used religious slogans, hoping that this would help to win over the mass of the peasantry who were still attached to the old religion. They declared that Elizabeth had established a 'new found religion and heresie, contrarie to God's word'. Even one of Elizabeth's rulers in the north stated that 'the ancient faith [Catholicism] still lay like lees at the bottom of men's hearts and if the vessel was ever so little stirred came to the top'. Although the rebellion was crushed easily, Haigh argues that it had posed a major challenge. It was only because the government acted effectively, by moving Mary Stuart away from the source of the rising so that she could not be a figurehead, that it survived. This view is supported by the fact that the government responded with over 450 executions and the seizure of large amounts of land. However, it would be fair to conclude that the rebellion stood little chance since Elizabeth had placed her own supporters in positions of power in the north and had a far stronger hold over the region than Henry had had in the 1530s.

Sir Francis Walsingham (1532–90)
He was a devout Protestant who had gone into exile during Mary's reign. During this time he gained a good understanding of European politics. In 1558, he returned and entered Parliament, and by 1573 he had become Secretary of State with special responsibility for foreign affairs. He was to become infamous for the spy ring that he established and the tortures he used to extract confessions from those suspected of plotting against Elizabeth.

Dutch Rebellion: the Netherlands was part of the Spanish Empire, but in 1572 a revolt broke out there. In part this was due to the growth of Calvinism, but constitutional, economic and social factors also played a part. Spanish armies were sent to put it down but failed, despite being the larger force. Most of the Dutch provinces saw fighting, but in the end it was the seven northern provinces that gained independence.

There was a series of plots involving attempts to assassinate Elizabeth and replace her with Mary Stuart, but although this might suggest that Catholicism was still a danger, most Catholics remained loyal to Elizabeth and were scandalised by Mary's involvement in plots against a fellow monarch. In many ways the plots helped to weaken Catholicism because they allowed the government to justify harsher measures against Catholics and to associate Catholicism with treasonous activities. The government spy ring, under the direction of **Sir Francis Walsingham**, ensured that these plots got nowhere and finally led to Mary's capture and execution, thus removing the Catholic alternative to Elizabeth. It can also be argued that the desperation of the plots shows how weak Catholicism was. The plotters realised that they lacked mass support and knew that the only way they could triumph was by the removal of Elizabeth.

Overseas support for Catholicism

There were also threats from Catholicism abroad, although this was only during the latter years of Elizabeth's reign. In Italy the papacy had failed to give English Catholics a lead until the Papal Bull, '*Regnans in Excelsis*' (The ruling of the Church), was issued in 1570. The leading European Catholic ruler, Philip II of Spain, was also unwilling to act against Elizabeth. Philip had his own difficulties at home with the **Dutch Rebellion** of 1566–1609 proving a constant problem and drain on resources. When France became caught up in its own Wars of Religion from 1562 it was also unable to help its co-religionists in England. Therefore it would appear that until 1570 the Catholic threat from overseas was minimal.

This position did not last, which was largely due to Elizabeth's own actions. By helping the Dutch rebels against Philip, Elizabeth had given Spain a reason to help English Catholics. This ill feeling between Spain and England culminated in the Armada of 1588 and a war that would continue until the end of her reign (this is discussed in greater detail on pp. 22–25). However, the defeat of the Armada was a great boost to Elizabeth, and may have convinced many Catholics that they had no choice but to accept her and her Church. To many contemporaries the defeat of the strongest nation in the world was a clear sign that England was God's chosen nation and this image was exploited in commemorative medals claiming 'God blew and they were scattered'.

How serious was the Puritan threat?

What is Puritanism?

In order to assess the threat posed by Puritanism it is necessary to be clear about the meaning of the term, yet this has caused controversy among historians. Patrick McGrath, in *Papists and Puritans under Elizabeth I* (1967), described them as those 'whose ideas and actions on matters concerning religious belief, religious practice, Church government or Church organisation brought them into conflict with the Church established by law and with the policy of the Supreme Governor'. Yet John Neale, in *The Elizabethan House of Commons* (1949), saw them as Protestants who were influenced by the Godly society of **Calvin's Geneva**. Others have used the term to mean 'left wing', 'fanatical' and 'very religious'. The Puritans themselves saw it as a term of abuse and preferred to use the label 'Godly', but despite the difficulties in agreeing on its meaning it has remained in use. At a very basic level it identifies those who wanted a simpler, more biblical form of worship and wanted to remove all elements of Catholicism from the Church. However, it is important not to talk of a Puritan 'group' because that term gives the impression of organisation, which was certainly not the case since there were several different strands and shades of opinion within the movement. Historians such as John Warren, in *Elizabeth I: Religion and Foreign Affairs* (1993), have identified three main strands of Puritan thought, each presenting a different challenge to Elizabeth. Probably the least significant threat came from the moderates: they reluctantly accepted the established Church, but worked within it to change both its structure and doctrine. The second group were the Presbyterians. They wanted a thorough reform of the Church, particularly the removal of bishops and their replacement with the Calvinist model of local, elected elders. This was unacceptable to a monarch who believed that the religious settlement of 1559 was final and that bishops were vital in upholding royal authority. It was probably this that caused Elizabeth to view all Puritans with suspicion. Finally there were the Separatists. This was the only element that looked to disband the national Church of the country and pursue its own reformation where each parish would decide its own direction. Despite this challenge, the threat they posed was limited because their numbers were so small. However, Elizabeth took a tough line against them, probably fearing that the movement could develop along similar lines to the **Anabaptist** movement in Germany and culminate in another **Munster**.

Calvin's Geneva: the city in Switzerland where John Calvin established his reformed Church. It was seen by many Protestants as being the model city.

Anabaptist: an extreme Protestant group who believed that baptism should only be administered to believing adults. Anabaptism was quite popular on the continent and worried authorities because of its radical social ideas, such as the common ownership of property and the taking of more than one wife.

Munster: anabaptists seized control of Munster in 1533–34. They drove out Lutherans, defied the Catholic Prince Bishop and announced a radical programme including infant baptism, polygamy and community of goods. Catholics and Lutherans fled the city. Whilst they ran the city sins made punishable by death included blasphemy, reviling parents, disobeying a master, adultery, spreading scandal and complaining. The Prince Bishop laid siege to the city, and by June 1535 most defenders had been butchered.

The lack of organisation and the presence of divisions within the Puritan movement weakened it from the very start. Unlike Catholics, the Puritans did not want to overthrow the monarch. Even if they did not agree with the religious settlement they preferred it to Elizabeth's removal and her replacement with the Catholic Mary Stuart. They were also desperate for Elizabeth to lead a European Protestant alliance against a resurgent Catholicism. Therefore, the challenge to Elizabeth was of a very different nature to that posed by Catholicism. According to some historians, the Puritan threat was to the **prerogative** Elizabeth held in religious matters, and in particular to the religious settlement.

Prerogative: the rights that the Queen enjoyed as feudal overlord and used to govern the kingdom. The Queen also claimed rights over the topics that could be debated in Parliament.

The challenge from within the Church of England

The first Puritan challenge came from within the Church. There were many clergy who did not regard the settlement of 1559 as the end of religious reform, but instead saw it as just the start. Many of the settlement's critics were the returning **Marian exiles** who had experienced Calvin's Geneva. They wanted to see a similar system established in England. Within a few months, as M. Knappen argued in *Tudor Puritanism* (1939), they were to face a harsh choice: either to accept the Queen's settlement or to adopt a policy of passive resistance. Many accepted positions within the new Church, some even accepting offers of bishoprics despite their views on Church government. Although some Puritans believed that these exiles had sold out, the exiles responded that it would be easier to reform the Church from within. Opponents maintained that they had weakened the Puritan movement and prevented it from developing links with fellow Calvinist communities in Europe.

Marian exiles: a term used to describe those Protestants who fled from England while Mary was on the throne, went to Protestant parts of Europe and returned under Elizabeth. They had often experienced radical religious reform whilst abroad and wanted the same thing to happen in England.

Vestments controversy: an argument caused by Puritan objections to the wearing of the correct dress by the clergy at services. Elizabeth insisted that correct dress was worn, but the Puritans saw this as 'the dress of Antichrist'.

Convocation: the Church's Parliament.

Advertisements: these laid down fixed rules for the conduct of services and the vestments that must be worn by clergy.

The scale of Puritan support within the Church was made very clear during the **Vestments controversy**. Puritan clergy had pushed for the removal of some elements of the new Church that they thought were too Catholic. Their petition was defeated in **Convocation** by only one vote. The struggle reached a climax in 1566 when the **Advertisements** laid down rules for the conduct of services and clerical dress. As a result of the rules, 37 clergy were removed from office and the Queen continued to insist that clergy wore the correct dress. Archbishop Parker tried to defuse the situation by persuading the Puritan clergy that their dress was based on ancient tradition. The problem of dress was symbolic of the wider Puritan concerns over issues such as holy days, the use of the sign of the cross, music and kneeling when receiving

Edmund Grindal (1519–83) Grindal had been chaplain to Edward VI, but went into exile under Mary, when he visited Protestant centres in Europe. He returned in 1558 and was appointed Bishop of London, then later Bishop of York. In 1576, he was made Archbishop of Canterbury. However, he came into conflict with Elizabeth because he refused to suppress prophesyings in 1577. He was suspended from office until his death in 1583.

communion. All of these were seen as legacies of Catholicism. Despite extensive opposition to these features of the Church, the Puritan campaign failed because Puritan bishops refused to resign over the issue of vestments, arguing that they could achieve more within the Church than outside it. This view was summed up by **Edmund Grindal**, later to become an Elizabethan archbishop, when he stated that clergy should not 'desert our churches for the sake of a few ceremonies and those not unlawful in themselves, especially since the pure doctrine of the gospel remained in all its integrity and freedom'. As a result there was division within the Puritan clergy over their approach to the religious settlement, which Elizabeth could exploit. Consequently the Puritan struggle shifted to Parliament so that leadership for the Puritan movement could be sought outside clerical circles.

William Strickland (d. 1598) A radical Puritan MP who, in 1571, tried to bring in proposals to reform the Prayer Book and remove those practices that were seen as Catholic. However, the Privy Council prevented him from attending Parliament and the bill was not passed.

Admonition to Parliament: a book attacking Church structure and doctrine, arguing that they were too similar to Catholic practices. The authors were imprisoned and many Puritan printing presses were destroyed.

Cope's 'Bill and Book': Anthony Cope, a Puritan MP, put forward his bill and new Prayer Book in 1587 to replace the existing Prayer Book with a more Calvinist version. His bill also proposed to establish a Genevan form of Church government where there were no bishops. Cope was sent to the Tower.

The 'Puritan Choir' and attempts to reform the Church through Parliament

The term 'Puritan Choir' was first used by John Neale in his book *Elizabeth I and her Parliaments* (Vol. 1, 1953; Vol. 2, 1957). According to Neale there was a significant group of MPs in Parliament who had forced Elizabeth into a more Protestant religious settlement than she wanted and had continued to agitate for further religious reform, a more active Protestant foreign policy and her marriage to safeguard a Protestant succession. Neale used a variety of events to show the strength of Puritan influence in Parliament. He cited examples such as when **William Strickland** introduced a bill to reform the Prayer Book in 1571, when the **Admonition to Parliament** was put forward in 1572 and when **Cope's 'Bill and Book'** calling for Parliament to discuss religious matters was moved in 1587.

However, this view has been challenged by Norman Jones, in his book *Faith by Statute* (1982), who has shown that the religious

Archbishop Whitgift (1530–1604)
He replaced Grindal as Archbishop of Canterbury in 1583. He supported Elizabeth's policy of enforcing uniformity, laying down regulations to improve clerical standards and ensuring that all clergy were loyal to Elizabeth. As a result of his policy, between 300 and 400 were removed.

Prorogue: the monarch had the right to suspend a parliamentary session until further notice.

Dissolve: Parliament could be dismissed and new elections would be needed before it could meet again.

Thirty Nine Articles: these constituted the definitive statement of the doctrine of the Elizabethan Church. Most were Calvinist in nature. Elizabeth refused to allow them to be confirmed by Parliament because they attacked many Catholic practices and thus would be likely to offend Catholics, even though she herself agreed with most of them.

settlement was not influenced by Puritans, but by the strength of Catholicism. Others have also shown that there was no organised Puritan 'group' and that attacks on the religious settlement were not sustained throughout the reign, only flaring up in response to particular events, such as **Archbishop Whitgift's** attack on 'godly preachers' in 1584. More importantly the influence of this 'group' was negligible. An examination of many of the conflicts shows how easy it was for Elizabeth to defeat the Puritan challenge. Elizabeth could use her prerogative to voice disapproval of any challenges, forbid discussion of certain issues, put members in gaol and ultimately, if the challenge continued, she could **prorogue**, suspend or **dissolve** Parliament. There were also other weapons available to her, particularly the influence of members of the Privy Council in the Commons. This happened in 1571 when they prevented Strickland from attending the Commons and in 1587 she was able to rely on them again when they denied MPs the opportunity to discuss Cope's Bill. It was not just the power of the monarch or her Council that meant that the Puritan parliamentary challenge stood little chance. There was also little support within Parliament for many of the measures. Elements of Puritanism threatened the established interests of the ruling class because they were direct challenges to stability and the social order. This was shown in 1584 when a speech by Sir Christopher Hatton ensured that a bill proposing to change Church government to a system similar to Geneva was lost.

Thus any review of the achievements of Puritanism within Parliament would have to conclude that it had failed. It is true that Puritans raised issues that were a direct challenge to Elizabeth's prerogative, but it is also probably fair to conclude that the publicity their attacks generated was far greater than their numbers warranted. No changes were made to the Church's organisation or hierarchy, which had been one of the major complaints of many Puritans, and the **Thirty Nine Articles** remained untouched. Clerical dress, especially the wearing of the surplice, a symbol of popish practice to many Puritans, remained and ministers had to conduct the service according to the prescribed manner of the Prayer Book.

Prophesyings and the local Puritan challenge

The failure of the Puritans to achieve their aims through Parliament resulted in a campaign on a local level. This campaign focused on two

Prophesyings: these were meetings of local clergy at which religious issues and topics were discussed. They gave many clergy the opportunity to improve their religious understanding and education. However, the government believed they were used to promulgate puritan ideas.

areas, **prophesyings** and classical Presbyterianism. Puritans believed that this was essential if they were to increase the number of good quality preachers and raise the overall standard of the clergy. However, as Patrick Collinson argues in *The Reign of Elizabeth I* (ed. Haigh, 1984), Elizabeth did not believe that any county needed more than three or four preachers apiece. She wanted them suppressed because they were outside her control and she believed that they encouraged unrest, bringing men 'to idleness and seduced and in a manner schismatically divided amongst themselves into variety of dangerous opinions and manifestly thereby encouraged to the violation of our laws and to the breach of common order'. But Archbishop Grindal refused to implement her request and argued that prophesyings actually helped to raise clerical standards. Elizabeth suspended Grindal, which meant that, until his death, the Church lacked an effective leader. As a result of her policy many Puritans became convinced that changes to the Church could only be achieved through secret local groups.

A satirical illustration showing how many Puritans viewed bishops. On the left the simply dressed cleric is holding a Bible (which they believed was at the centre of religion and the only way to reach God). The other two figures are lavishly dressed, more like Catholics. One is holding a Prayer Book and the other an old book containing superstitions — seen by Puritans as of less value in the search for salvation, and even the work of the devil. The picture is an attack on the old values, which bishops were still seen to uphold.

This belief found its outlet in classical Presbyterianism, which represented a serious threat to Elizabeth. Groups of local clergy met together in secret and corresponded with other groups, both at home and overseas. Not only was a strong network established, but the movement's desire to reorganise the Church structure along Calvinist lines was a direct challenge to the Queen's view that Church government was solely the responsibility of the state.

However, the challenge was short-lived; with Grindal's death in 1583, Elizabeth was able to appoint Whitgift as the new archbishop of Canterbury. He was more than willing to carry out Elizabeth's wishes because he had no sympathy with Puritanism. By forcing clergy to swear an acceptance of bishops, the Prayer Book and the Thirty Nine Articles he was able to identify those who did not defer to the settlement. Thus over 300 clergy in the south were suspended within a short space of time, although many were later reinstated. Whitgift's strict controls ensured that uniformity was enforced. Historians are agreed that his contribution was vital in destroying the Presbyterian threat and in ensuring that Presbyterianism would have to be practised in secret if it was to continue.

The Separatist challenge

It was obvious by the 1580s that the Puritans could not bring about reform from within the Church. Whitgift's efforts had broken the back of the movement and driven what remained of it underground. Those who wanted to continue to pursue their own religious beliefs would have to do it outside the established Church. Although it is difficult to be certain about the strength and numbers of the remaining group, because their activities were illegal and therefore remained secret, it is unlikely that their numbers were very great. The government was concerned because these Puritans practised their religion in secret and were outside their control. However, they drew a disproportionate amount of attention from the authorities because the government was determined to make an example of them and dissuade others from following a similar route. The government had great success in destroying their printing presses and imprisoned many Puritan leaders, including Robert Browne, and executed others for distributing Browne's work.

Perhaps the greatest Separatist challenge came in 1589 with the publication of the **Marprelate Tracts**. This work soon became a best-seller and might have worried the government because of its popular support. However, in the long term the impact was negative

Marprelate Tracts: a series of pamphlets produced by the Separatists in 1589.

because the government used this incident to link all Puritans with the Separatist movement and treason. This led to the government passing the 1593 **Act against Seditious Sectaries** which was aimed at anyone suspected of being a Separatist. Therefore, not only was the Separatist challenge successfully dealt with, but the government was able to use it to portray all Puritans as subversive at a time when national unity was required in the war against Spain.

Act against Seditious Sectaries: this act of 1593 punished those who refused to attend church or persuaded others not to attend, and those who denied the Queen's authority in religious matters. It was aimed at the Separatist movement.

The decline of Puritanism

It was not only the attack on the Separatists and its wider consequences that seriously weakened the Puritan movement in the 1590s. In the last years of Elizabeth's reign, the death of many influential Puritans, such as Leicester and Warwick, weakened the cause further. They had given Puritanism a mouthpiece at court, but without them its influence would wane. Perhaps it was Elizabeth herself who, by her refusal to make any further reforms after the settlement, had created the Puritan danger and made it a greater threat than it need have been. However, before completely dismissing the threat it posed, it must not be forgotten that Puritanism had not been eradicated from English thought and would be a significant factor in the outbreak of the English Civil War (1640–47).

Which was the greater threat Catholicism or Puritanism?

The threat presented by Catholicism and Puritanism changed during the period. At first, the greater threat appeared to come from Catholics at home, as they outnumbered Protestants, and this can be seen in the settlement of 1559. Many Catholics ultimately wanted to remove Elizabeth and replace her with Mary Stuart. The Puritans, on the other hand, although they wanted a more radical religious settlement, did not want to overthrow Elizabeth to see her replaced by a Catholic.

However, later in the reign, the Catholic threat at home decreased. Few were prepared to rise against Elizabeth, as was seen by the failure of the rising of the Northern Earls in 1569 and the lack of support for the Armada. Forced into a choice, after Elizabeth's excommunication, most put their nation first. The Puritan threat was always limited as most merely challenged the assumptions and aims of Elizabeth. The threat in Parliament was always contained and little was achieved by the 'Puritan Choir'. However, the Separatist challenge, despite the small numbers, was a challenge. Their assumptions were subversive and they did offer an alternative Church order, but even they would rather have Elizabeth on the throne than Mary Stuart.

Therefore, it may be argued that the greatest challenge came from overseas Catholic powers. There was a possibility of a Franco-Spanish crusade and even the plots presented a mortal and immediate threat to Elizabeth. An invasion, even if it did not remove Elizabeth, was liable to overthrow the order she had established and plunge the country into civil war. Although the benefit of hindsight allows us to see that this did not happen, it did appear a serious possibility on a number of occasions.

Who presented Elizabeth with the greater threat: Catholics or Puritans?

1. Read the following extract and answer the question.

'The number of Catholics, thank God, is daily increasing here, owing to the College and seminary for Englishmen which your Majesty [Philip II] ordered to be supported in Douai, from where there has come in the last year a hundred Englishmen who have been ordained there, by which means a great number of people are being converted, generally persons who have never heard the truth preached before. These priests go about disguised as laymen, and although they are young men, their good life, fervency and zeal in their work are admirable.'

(report from the *Spanish State Papers*, 28 December 1579)

Using the information in this book and your own knowledge, how accurate is this account in describing the success of the Catholic missionary movement in England?

2. Assess the success of Elizabeth's religious policy towards either Catholics or Puritans.

3

How much power did Elizabeth's Parliament have?

How did Elizabeth
control Parliament?

What was the role
of Parliament in the
16th century?

Was there conflict
between her and
Parliament?

Framework of Events

1558	William Cecil appointed Permanent Secretary
1559	First parliamentary session: religious settlement agreed
1563	Second parliamentary session: disagreements occur over Elizabeth's marriage and the succession
1566	Third parliamentary session: disagreements over marriage and the succession continue
1571	Fourth parliamentary session: further disputes over the succession arise
	William Cecil is created Lord Burghley
1572	Fifth parliamentary session: disagreements take place over Mary Stuart and the Duke of Norfolk
1576	Wentworth is imprisoned for demanding greater freedom of speech
1584	Parliament and Elizabeth differ again about the succession
1587	Wentworth makes another speech arguing for freedom of speech
1597	Twelfth parliamentary session: discontent is voiced over monopolies
1601	Elizabeth's last Parliament: she makes the 'Golden Speech'

Democracy: a form of government in which the country is ruled by Parliament and each person in the country has a vote to elect an MP. In the 16th century this idea would have been considered absurd. Only those with substantial property might have had the right to choose an MP.

PERHAPS the greatest debate among historians studying the reign of Elizabeth I has concerned the development of Parliament as an institution. Study of this subject first began in the 19th century, when England was moving towards a **democracy** and writers were looking for its origins. They saw the first tentative steps taking place in the Elizabethan period. In the 20th century, the debate centred around the works of Sir John Neale, particularly his books *The Elizabethan House of Commons* (1949) and *Elizabeth I and her Parliaments* (Vol. 1, 1953; Vol. 2 1957). In his view, Parliament was the centre of disputes and division between a conservative monarch, who was determined to preserve her prerogative, and an organised group of MPs leading an aggressive and radical Commons, who wanted to assert and increase **parliamentary privileges** and powers. Neale believed that many of these conflicts concerned the question of religion. This interpretation was accepted by many historians who saw the struggle of the latter years of Charles I's reign, when the **English Civil War** broke out, beginning under Elizabeth. However, more recently this view has been challenged and historians such as Michael Graves, in *Elizabethan Parliaments 1559–1601* (1987), have shown that Parliament was much more co-operative than Neale believed.

Parliamentary privileges: the rights given to MPs once they were elected. There were disputes between Elizabeth and MPs as to how far these rights, which included the controversial topics of free speech and freedom from arrest, extended. The rights were usually requested by the Speaker at the opening session of Parliament and the Crown had repeatedly granted them. However, the clash was between these privileges and the Crown's prerogative over certain issues.

English Civil War: war broke out when the King and his supporters fought against Parliament and lasted from 1642–47.

How did Elizabeth control Parliament?

Elizabeth's personality

According to many historians, Elizabeth's most important weapon in controlling and managing Parliament was her own personality. At times her mere presence in Parliament was enough to stifle criticism. It might seem strange that the Queen attended debates and influenced the outcome by her presence, but this was an age when the monarch was expected to play more than a **ceremonial role**. Few people at the time would have questioned her right to influence Parliament, and those who did would be viewed with suspicion. Her speeches were carefully written to persuade, cajole or threaten MPs, but chiefly, according to Haigh, to 'stand on her considerable dignity, reminding peers and MPs that they were her subjects and she was their Queen chosen by God'. This ability to charm the House was seen most clearly perhaps in the **'Golden Speech'** of 1601, in which she used many of the techniques that characterised her management of Parliament throughout her reign. She spoke of her love for her people and said that she put her people before herself. Finally she moved on to deal with the critical issue of monopolies. In this instance she deflected the blame from herself

Ceremonial role: today the monarchy has only a very limited amount of power, but carries out public duties on formal occasions. However, in the 16th century the monarch was expected to be active in political decision-making.

'Golden Speech': a speech made by Elizabeth to her last Parliament of 1601 in which she talked of her love for her subjects and the country. It was first given this name when historians saw her reign as a golden age and viewed this speech as a fitting climax to it.

saying that 'If my kingly bounties have been abused, and my grants turned to the hurt of my people, contrary to my will and meaning, and if any authority under me have neglected or perverted what I have committed to them, I hope God will not lay their culps and offences to my charge'. Her speech was received well, which was a sign that, even at the end of her reign, when many historians accept that opposition was growing, she could still count on the support of the political nation. It would therefore be hard to argue that there was serious conflict between the Queen and Parliament.

The use of messages and rumours

Elizabeth also used messages to exercise her authority. If she was unable to attend Parliament, she could use those councillors who had seats in the Commons to direct debates and explain her wishes. Her intervention could be direct, leaving no doubt about what she wanted. However, it is interesting that there is little evidence of complaint when this happened, which suggests that the Commons was not as assertive as Neale thought. It appears that most MPs believed that the monarch had the right to tell them what could be discussed.

Elizabeth also used the technique of a 'whispered rumour', whereby a rumour indicating the Queen's wishes was spread about the chamber. Naturally, it is difficult for the historian to find out how often it was used and whether it was actually the monarch who started the rumour. At other times Elizabeth was more direct and summoned the **Speaker** so that she could explain what she wanted and have it reported to the Commons.

Speaker: an elected official in the House of Commons whose job it is to control debates and procedure to ensure that the rules of the House are obeyed.

Veto: the Queen's right to reject bills and thus prevent them from becoming law.

Arrest and veto

If her words failed to stop criticism, Elizabeth possessed the ultimate weapons of arrest and **veto**. The power of arrest was witnessed in 1576, when an MP, Peter Wentworth, was sent to the Tower for demanding freedom of speech in the Commons. However, it was not the Queen who ordered the arrest, but the MPs. The Commons' decision to act illustrates that many members did not want to offend the Queen and that her powers of control were seldom needed because members would regulate issues themselves.

Neale argued that, when Elizabeth used the veto, she was on the defensive, forced to use this weapon to block parliamentary legislation that she did not like, thereby causing conflict with Parliament. However, a closer examination of the occasions when Elizabeth used the veto suggests otherwise. It is difficult to be sure, because parliamentary records for the latter part of

Elizabeth's reign have been lost, but its use in the early part of her reign would not suggest that she was fighting an aggressive lower chamber. It seems that the veto was used more frequently to block poorly drafted legislation because many **bills** that had been vetoed became law in later sessions, once they had been redrafted. Elizabeth also used the veto to block legislation that damaged the interests of particular groups who had not been consulted when the initial bills were drawn up. There are only five instances of the Queen using the veto to block legislation she disliked. Three of these instances concerned moves to make the Church more Protestant and two concerned debates about Mary Stuart when Elizabeth still wished to protect her. Therefore, although Elizabeth could control Parliament with her powers of veto and arrest, she rarely used them because the relationship between monarch and Parliament was usually good.

Bill: the draft form of a law, before it becomes an Act.

William Cecil, Lord Burghley (1520–98)
He was born in 1520 into the gentry. He served Edward VI, but retired when Mary became Queen. When Elizabeth came to the throne she appointed him Secretary of State. He became probably the most well-known of all her ministers and worked with Elizabeth for most of her reign. Much of his work was concerned with financial management. In 1571, he was created Lord Burghley, and in 1582 he became Lord Treasurer. He was promoted because of his ability, and tended to be a cautious man who wanted to avoid religious extremism, be it from Catholics or Puritans. He wanted to ensure England remained independent by avoiding war abroad, which brought him into conflict with Leicester, who favoured an anti-Spanish policy. He died in 1598.

The role of councillors

Until the 1590s, Parliament was largely under the control of Elizabeth's councillors. They ensured that parliamentary business was under their control, drew up agendas and managed debates so that the royal will was usually achieved. They also saw to it that the Commons had less freedom of speech and cut down the time allowed for speeches. This control meant that there were times when councillors used their influence to direct Parliament in the way that they, rather than the monarch, wished. This occurred in 1571 when they pressured Elizabeth, through MPs in the Commons, to exclude Mary Stuart from succession.

The Queen also relied on the support of **William Cecil**, later Lord Burghley, to manage Parliament. At first he achieved this through the Commons, where he was a member. Graves showed that he 'drafted memoranda on official objectives, masterminded the government's legislative programmes, drafted bills and promoted others he liked'. He sat on as many committees as possible so that he could put forward the royal view. Whenever he spoke, particularly to oppose measures, he ensured that his arguments had been well researched. For example, when he asked for money for Elizabeth, he stressed how much of her own she had already spent. The Commons was the more important of the two houses in the early period, simply because Cecil was present there and used it to introduce government-backed legislation. However, in 1571, when Cecil moved to the Lords, he had to

NON SINE SOLE
IRIS

This portrait of Elizabeth (c. 1600) is loaded with symbolism, and would have been immensely flattering. The Queen's cloak is decorated with tiny eyes and ears, suggesting the way the Queen used her councillors to see and hear for her within Parliament. There is a coiled serpent on her left sleeve, symbolising prudence, and on the bodice are embroidered spring flowers, indicative of the new century which was just beginning. The rainbow is the traditional symbol of peace.

Landmark Study   The book that changed people's views

Geoffrey Elton, *The Parliament of England 1559–1581* (Cambridge University Press, 1986)

Although best known for his work on Tudor government under Henry VIII, Elton's book on the Elizabethan Parliament was crucial in challenging and undermining the hitherto accepted orthodoxy of the historian Sir John Neale. Elton challenged Neale in two main areas. Firstly, he argued that, contrary to Neale, the House of Lords was a more important institution than the House of Commons in the Elizabethan age. More importantly for subsequent historians, Elton's work challenged the assumption that the Commons was assertive and anti-government and showed that there was much more evidence of co-operation than Neale had led us to believe. Elton argued that Parliament voted subsidies, debated and passed bills with little trouble and sorted out many local issues, such as land ownership. He concluded that parliamentary sessions usually ended harmoniously and that the government saw the required legislation passed. Elton's work was also important because it successfully challenged the argument that the origins of the English Civil War could be found in the Commons-led opposition of the Elizabethan period. This made historians re-examine the long-term causes of the conflict and, as a result of Elton's work, Neale's well-established interpretation collapsed quickly.

Commonweal matters: issues that concerned the best interests of everyone in the country.

Private bills: draft legislation that was introduced by MPs, rather than the government.

Boroughs: towns with royal charters that gave them the right to send two MPs to Parliament.

modify his management techniques. Elton refers to this as a 'new form of conciliar control, called into existence by the departure to the House of Lords of the manager-in-chief' (see **Landmark Study**, above). Cecil wrote memoranda giving instructions and applied pressure to the Commons. He sent many messages telling the Commons to concentrate on **Commonweal matters**, to put aside **private bills**, to arrange bills in order of priority and to give precedence to subsidies. Graves concludes that the Lords maintained 'relentless pressure and the Commons, perhaps surprisingly, responded to it in a positive and constructive manner'.

The councillors also had a lot of influence over who should be chosen as MPs. Councillors often wrote to local officials such as JPs, Lord Lieutenants and Sheriffs, to recommend people or to give instructions on the supervision of elections so that desirable people were returned. Once elected, these MPs awaited a lead from the Council members in the Commons and were willing to follow. Many councillors, such as Lord Burghley who was responsible for returning 26 MPs in 1584, had influence in certain **boroughs** and could ensure that their nominees were returned. This meant that Elizabeth could guarantee a substantial core of support and that the councillors' influence increased.

The role of the Speaker

Elizabeth also influenced the choice of Speaker. Although he was formally elected by the Commons, he was a Crown nominee. This was important because he controlled debates, directed the order of business and could direct the Commons as the Queen wanted.

Those councillors who were also MPs provided him with advice and 'whispered rumours' so that he knew Elizabeth's wishes. It was comments from councillors that prompted the Speaker to warn the Commons in 1581 about 'unnecessary motions or superfluous arguments'.

The House of Lords

House of Lords: the upper house, consisting of peers and bishops.

Burghley's promotion to the **House of Lords** changed the balance of importance between the two houses back in favour of the upper house, which undermines the Neale thesis about the growing power of the Commons. If the Commons had become as powerful as Neale suggested, it is unlikely that Elizabeth would have moved her manager from the Commons to the Lords at the very time he was needed in the lower house. When Burghley became a member of the Lords, the amount of business that started there increased significantly. At the same time, the Lords brought pressure to bear on the lower house when necessary. It gave the Crown the support of its collective **social weight** and of its control over many of its clients in the Commons. However, there was not complete harmony within the Lords. There were differences of opinion between Burghley and Leicester, and between Whitgift and the more Puritan lords, but Burghley and Whitgift were usually able to persuade the House to follow their lead.

Social weight: the influence and status of the Lords was sometimes important in persuading the Commons to accept certain pieces of legislation.

The attitude of MPs

It is clear that the Queen used several methods to control Parliament. All of them were used to varying degrees and at different times, but they were acceptable to most MPs. Those who did object, like Wentworth, were the exception. This suggests that there was no reason for Elizabeth to dislike calling Parliament. In fact, it seems that it was the MPs who disliked being summoned. An examination of the records shows that attendance was never good and declined as the length of the sessions increased. It became so bad that procedures to fine and punish those who were absent were introduced. Members objected to the cost of staying in London for long periods and to being absent from their businesses or estates. They also did not regard Parliament as a particularly significant political event. An average of ten MPs spoke in debates, and under half of them bothered to vote, which suggests that most material was not controversial. This was because most legislation concerned local issues. Most MPs wanted the sessions to be over as quickly as possible, but this is where there could be conflict between Elizabeth and Parliament. She wanted the session to finish once money had been granted, but the MPs wanted to deal with local issues that concerned them, which delayed government business.

What was the role of Parliament in the 16th century?

Parliament in the 16th century was unlike its modern equivalent. During the reign of Henry VIII, as a result of the break with Rome and the need to legalise the changes, the role of Parliament had developed considerably. Development continued under Edward and Mary, because Parliament was used to enact further **religious changes**. As Graves argued, Parliament had been involved in 'the highest matters of state, altered both religion and ecclesiastical organisation, encroached upon property rights in a drastic manner, and legislated on all aspects of the Commonweal'. It was a well-established institution by the time Elizabeth came to the throne, but it had not become more powerful. It met for only 13 sessions in the 45 years of Elizabeth's reign and no session lasted for more than a few months. Neale has suggested that this was because Elizabeth disliked Parliament and that her relationship with it was strained. Elizabeth had the right to summon, prorogue or dissolve Parliament whenever she wanted. Neale argued that she used this right on many occasions and had to be persuaded to summon Parliament, which happened only when she wanted financial help. There were also limits, due to custom and practice, as to what Parliament could discuss. Issues such as religion, foreign policy, money, marriage and the succession were all considered to be under royal prerogative and therefore were not to be debated. Unlike today, there were no political parties, although there were loose groupings due to family connections and friendships. Consequently, Parliament played a peripheral role in the government of the country. Instead government was carried out by the Privy Council, which was responsible to the Queen.

However, summoning Parliament gave Elizabeth a valuable opportunity to have contact with her subjects and to listen to their concerns. Her speeches indicate that she used Parliament to explain royal policies to MPs so that they would be more likely to implement them when they returned to their counties. Parliament was also vital for the raising of taxes. Alan Smith, in *The Government of Elizabethan England* (1967), has pointed out that in 11 of the 13 parliamentary sessions the government asked for money. However, Parliament was not seen simply as a means of obtaining taxes. Elizabeth allowed time for other business, which

Religious changes: under Edward and Mary England underwent a series of religious changes that saw England become fully Protestant under Edward and then restored to the Catholic faith and papal supremacy under Mary. Parliament was responsible for passing the laws that brought about these changes.

A contemporary drawing of Elizabeth and her Parliament. Elizabeth is seated at the head and raised on a platform under a canopy to reflect her royal status. The Lords are also seated and the Commons standing (as still happens today), a further reflection of status.

MPs used to raise matters of concern and to deal with pressing local issues. Most of the Commons' work involved legislation on uncontentious issues, creating an outlet for local matters to be resolved quickly. Parliament was seen as a valuable part of the running of the country and there is no evidence to suggest that Elizabeth ever thought of dismantling it.

Was there conflict between Elizabeth and Parliament?

The Neale debate

According to Neale, the power of the Commons increased throughout Elizabeth's reign. He argued that the new, rising class of university-educated gentry saw the parliamentary sessions as an opportunity to discuss the great issues of the day, such as religion and the succession. He maintained that there was an organised opposition, which he called the 'Puritan Choir', who increasingly challenged Elizabeth's control, formalising the procedure of the house and asserting parliamentary privilege, thus increasing the power of the Commons. Neale's evidence for the existence of this group was a 1566 pamphlet that named 43 such MPs. He then cited occasions when these MPs had challenged Elizabeth's wishes, such as the conflict over the **Norfolk election** in 1586 when the Commons asserted its right to settle election disputes. He argued that the 'Puritan Choir' deliberately planned confrontations with the Queen to raise the issue of parliamentary privilege against the royal prerogative.

Norfolk election: the House of Commons asserted its right to settle a disputed election in the county of Norfolk, although this was usually done by the Lord Chancellor.

After many years, Neale's interpretation was challenged by Elton in *The Parliaments of England 1559–1581* (1986). Where Neale had concentrated on parliamentary conflicts, Elton looked at Parliament's legislative achievements. He argued that Parliament usually dealt effectively with raising money, passing bills and resolving local issues. He accepted that there were clashes, but argued that these were simply part of the debating process and that Parliament usually ended on a harmonious note.

Elton also challenged Neale's concept of the 'Puritan Choir', arguing that this group was less united and powerful than Neale proposed. It failed to bring about any religious changes, which suggests that it lacked power over legislation. There is evidence that some of those named in the 1566 pamphlet were not Puritans: some were possibly the Queen's councillors, or their followers, and others even had Catholic leanings. When Parliament challenged the Queen it was generally because they had been instructed to do so by the councillors, who wanted to exert pressure on Elizabeth. Furthermore, there is debate about the purpose of the 1566 pamphlet. It seems that those named were members of a committee that consulted the Lords on issues of common concern, since the same number of MPs served on the committee as Neale named as members of the choir. However, there is still no agreement as to why this satirical attack on the committee was published, particularly at a time of high printing costs.

More recent work by Haigh and Graves supported Elton, and most historians now agree that Elizabeth's relationship with Parliament was more harmonious than Neale suggests. Graves concludes that 'the revisionists have convincingly rejected the notion that the Commons' political muscle and ... opposition to royal government increased, and especially that organised opposition was a regular feature of the Elizabethan lower house. They have restored to a prominent place the House of Lords, whose institutional authority was augmented by the presence of so many **patrons** with kin and clients in the lower house'.

Patrons: members of the Lords who, through their power and influence, controlled the election of MPs to certain seats in the House of Commons. This meant that the MP was under the control and influence of his patron.

The religious issue

Neale argued that the religious issue was a major battleground in Parliament because the 'Puritan Choir' wanted to make changes to the 1559 religious settlement. He maintains that the conflict started in 1559, when Puritans had forced Elizabeth to accept a more radical religious settlement than she wanted. Conflict continued throughout 1563–67, and in 1566, for the first time, Parliament refused to grant taxation until their grievances were met. Although they failed this time, the strategy was used successfully in the 1640s. In the 1570s, the 'Puritan Choir' gained radical leaders and raised further radical religious demands, centred on the Admonition to Parliament. Discontent continued during the 1570s, when there was increased pressure for a change to the religious settlement. During the 1580s, the Puritans launched their campaign to replace the Prayer Book and the present system of Church government with a more Calvinist approach. Neale argued that this opposition was well organised and that opponents met beforehand to plan tactics, which caused the government significant difficulties.

However, more recent work by Norman Jones in *Faith by Statute* (1982) challenged Neale and showed that there was no evidence of a cohesive Puritan pressure group in the Commons. Although the

Puritan campaign to dismantle the Elizabethan settlement was vociferous, it was led by only a handful of members. According to Graves, they lacked the support of most members, making it easy for Elizabeth to defeat them. Support for the Puritan cause was so weak that Parliament refused even to hear **Turner's Bill** to change the Prayer Book. Jones argued that the greatest pressure for change came from the Catholics in the House of Lords. This interpretation is supported by Elizabeth's actions. She imprisoned two bishops after they had a dispute with Protestants and when all but one bishop refused to accept the settlement they were replaced (see pp. 31–32 for more details on the religious issue).

Turner's Bill: a Member of Parliament, Dr Peter Turner, introduced a bill in Parliament in 1584 which would have established a national Presbyterian Church, but the Queen vetoed this by preventing the commons from discussing religious matters.

Marriage and the succession

The members of the 'Puritan Choir' are seen by Neale as organising the resistance to Elizabeth's refusal to marry or name a successor. The central figure in this conflict was Peter Wentworth. When Elizabeth reminded the house of her status and forbade further discussion of her marriage and succession, he responded by demanding freedom of speech in the Commons so that any subject could be discussed.

The first session of the 1570s happened just after the Northern Earls' Revolt and, according to Neale, the 'Puritan Choir' led calls for the execution of the **Duke of Norfolk** and Mary Stuart. They persuaded Elizabeth to execute Norfolk and to consider excluding Mary from the succession. However, the greatest clash of the decade came in 1576 when Wentworth once again demanded freedom of speech on all issues. Elizabeth sent him to the Tower but, according to Neale, by this time Wentworth had become the champion of Parliament's struggle to gain its privileges against a conservative monarch. Many MPs supported his beliefs and felt that the Commons was the best place for issues such as religion, foreign policy and the succession to be discussed. It is clear that there was substantial discontent over the Queen's failure to marry, or name a successor, in the 1560s and 1570s.

Duke of Norfolk (1536–72)
He was a very powerful noble and had a great deal of influence in local and central government. He owned vast estates and his tenants were usually loyal supporters, making him a potential threat to the Crown. His power meant that he controlled the Norfolk Commission of the Peace and appointed over half of the county's JPs. He also had a lot of patronage available to him, including seats in the Commons. He was the senior noble in the realm and in 1568–69 it was planned to marry him to Mary Stuart. This plan had the support of Leicester who wanted to see the influence of Cecil reduced. The plan was discovered and Norfolk fled. He begged the Queen for mercy, but was imprisoned and later executed.

The councillors

Revisionist historians have suggested that where there is evidence of conflict between Elizabeth and Parliament, it is because Parliament was being used by Elizabeth's own ministers, who were frustrated at their inability to achieve their aims through discussions within the Privy Council. Therefore, they used

Sir Francis Knollys (c. 1514–96)
He was a relative of Anne Boleyn and had held office under Edward. He was appointed to Elizabeth's council in 1558. He was a devout Protestant and often tried to persuade the Queen to follow a more Protestant foreign policy, which explains his involvement in calls to exclude Mary Stuart from the succession and finally execute her.

Sir James Croft (c. 1520–90)
The head of a leading family on the Welsh borders, he was implicated in Wyatt's rebellion of 1554 to remove Mary Tudor and replace her with Elizabeth. He was appointed a councillor in 1566. However, despite this earlier evidence of Protestant ardour he was a conservative in religious issues and pro-Spanish. Although he led the Commons in calls for the execution of Mary Stuart, by the late 1580s he was selling secrets to the Spanish and negotiating with Parma while the Armada was on its way. The fact that he was allowed to do this suggests that Elizabeth was never wholeheartedly committed to a policy of war. He died in 1590, another of the 'old guard' of Elizabeth's councillors to depart in that last decade.

Early Stuart rulers: James I and Charles I who ruled England between 1603 and 1649.

Parliament to generate popular support for their view and pressurise Elizabeth into changing her mind. In the 1560s, having failed in Privy Council discussions to persuade Elizabeth to marry, councillors raised the issue in Parliament. The Council had been worried when a bout of smallpox almost killed Elizabeth in 1563, and a parliamentary committee containing all the councillors in the Commons was established to draft a petition to the Queen. Councillors repeated their approaches regarding the execution of Mary Stuart and the supply of aid to the Dutch rebels. The campaign to exclude Mary from the throne was led by **Sir Francis Knollys** and **Sir James Croft**, both of whom were councillors. Later it was the Queen's Secretary, Lord Burghley, who encouraged the debates, hoping that, if Parliament expressed its disapproval with policy, Elizabeth would change her mind.

Growing conflict and monopolies

Opposition to religious policy continued in the 1580s as the Puritans launched their campaign to replace both the Prayer Book and the present system of Church government with a more Calvinist approach. Neale argued that this opposition was well organised and that opponents met beforehand to plan tactics which caused the government significant difficulties. The Commons also asserted their right to settle election disputes when, in 1586, there was conflict over the Norfolk election (see p. 54). Opposition was becoming more co-ordinated and successful in asserting parliamentary privilege.

According to Neale, the conflict reached a crisis over monopolies. In both 1598 and 1601 Elizabeth had called Parliament in order to obtain money for the war against Spain. However, the opposition hijacked the sessions and forced Elizabeth into making compromises. There was an organised rebellion by her critics, as they believed that she had misused her prerogative in granting monopolies and thus raising the price of goods. In such a climate, the Commons also claimed the right to initiate any vote for money and therefore voted only a fraction of the government's request. The growing power of the Commons, according to Neale, is shown by the fact that although Elizabeth initially ignored the complaints, she was forced into cancelling some of the monopolies and investigating others. Therefore, her reign ended with increasing opposition that was able to force her into making serious concessions, a forerunner of the problems that would face **early Stuart rulers** in their dealings with Parliament.

It would certainly be wrong to abandon the idea of conflict when examining the 1590s, when the Queen had to use all her skills and personal charm to diffuse discontent over monopolies. Revisionist historians, such as Alan Smith, writing in *The Government of Elizabethan England* (1967) have explained why the 1590s saw a much more turbulent relationship between the monarch and Parliament. He has shown that the government was gradually losing the control it had once held over the Commons. In part, this was because the leading councillors, who had sat in the Commons and managed parliamentary business for the monarch, had either died or were now too old. At the same time, **parliamentary committees** were starting to seize the initiative and were becoming more involved in putting forward new policies, rather than examining legislation that had been drafted by councillors. Finally, it was the crown's financial predicament, caused largely by war with Spain, which gave the commons a greater voice. In order to obtain the money needed, the government was forced to pay greater attention to the complaints and demands of the members of the lower house. As the revisionist historian Graves has argued, this is an example of rising discontent, 'a spontaneous response to a common grievance, voiced by the governing class through its representatives'.

Parliamentary committees: these were committees set up by MPs outside royal control to draft petitions on issues they wanted the monarch to address. Usually they concerned the succession, Elizabeth's marriage and parliamentary privileges.

Recent historical developments

Recent studies have stressed the harmonious relationship that the Queen enjoyed with her Parliaments. Historians such as Graves have shown that, when there were clashes, they were of no long-term significance, largely because the opposition was neither organised nor strong enough to present a serious challenge to the Queen. More recently historians such as Elton have stressed the role of the House of Lords, rather than the Commons, in initiating legislation. This was particularly true after 1571, when Cecil moved to the Lords as Lord Burghley. Many of the members of the upper house had such powers of **patronage** that they were able to control or influence members of the Commons and ensure that they did their bidding, thereby limiting the independence of the lower house.

Patronage: the rewarding of supporters with titles, wealth or jobs in the hope that they would remain loyal.

The revisionist approach, particularly that of Elton, has largely been the result of studying Parliament in a much wider context than Neale. As a result, it is probably fair to conclude that the relationship between Elizabeth and Parliament was normally amicable. There are examples of conflict, but these are not typical. Secondly, much greater prominence must be given to the role of the

House of Lords. Lastly, the attempts that Neale identified as the Commons trying to extend its power, were in fact the Commons reacting on the spur of the moment to events and realising that its position was weak and needed defending.

 How much power did Elizabeth's Parliament have?

1. Read the following extract and answer the question.

> *'For the most time there was no need for any but the gentlest management to ensure that business was completed. But sometimes there was trouble, and, from Elizabeth's point of view, it was more serious than Neale thought. For the trouble was not usually between Elizabeth's government and her Parliament, it was between Elizabeth herself and her government and Parliament in alliance.'*

(Christopher Haigh, *Elizabeth I*, Longman, 1988, p. 118)

Using your own knowledge, how adequately does the extract above describe Elizabeth's relations with her Parliament?

2. How successful was Elizabeth's management of Parliament?

Elizabeth I: an assessment

Foreign Policy

Elizabeth had limited resources available to her and was often forced simply to respond to circumstances. However, she protected national security and prevented invasion. The threat posed by France or Spain gaining control of the Netherlands was negated and the border with Scotland was secured.

Religion

The religious settlement of 1559 satisfied neither Catholics nor Puritans. Catholicism survived in England after the settlement, but became a minority religion that was confined mainly to the gentry, despite attempts by the government to suppress it. Meanwhile, the Puritans failed to bring about any radical reform of the Church and alter the religious settlement. By the end of Elizabeth's reign the Anglican Church was firmly established, Catholicism had been reduced to a sect and Puritans who had challenged the settlement in Parliament had been silenced.

Parliament

Parliament was, by the end of the Elizabethan period, an established part of government. The relationship between the Queen and Parliament was usually good. There were disputes over her marriage and the succession, but they happened when the Privy Council agreed with Parliament rather than with the Queen. Most MPs knew that there were certain topics that could not be discussed and harmony was preserved by careful management.

Elizabeth's legacy

Although the last decade of Elizabeth's reign witnessed many problems, the experience of the early Stuarts and the Civil War soon ensured that her popularity recovered. The image of a 'Golden Age' may lack some substance, but it is a clear sign of Elizabeth's remarkable popularity. Her reign had shown that it was possible for a female ruler not only to survive, but to flourish, in a male-dominated world. Her legacy is still present today. The Anglican Church was firmly established by the end of her reign and the first steps towards an overseas empire had been made as England moved from being a second-rate nation to a maritime power. The government had increased its sphere of influence over people's lives and the Elizabethan Poor Laws saw the state take on new responsibilities, ensuring that, during the crisis years of the last decade, hunger did not lead to widespread rebellion. However, perhaps Elizabeth's greatest legacy was the cultural development of the period, which saw the emergence of some of the nation's greatest playwrights, artists and poets.

Further reading

Texts specifically designed for students

Doran, S. *England and Europe 1485–1603* (Longman, 1986)
Doran, S. *Elizabeth I and Religion 1558–1603* (Routledge, 1994)
Mervyn, B. *The Reign of Elizabeth I* (John Murray, 2001)
Randell, K. *Elizabeth I and the Government of England* (Hodder, 1994)
Warren, J. *Elizabeth I: Religion and Foreign Affairs* (Hodder, 1993)

Texts for more advanced study

Elton, G. *The Parliament of England 1559–1581* (Cambridge University Press, 1986) was the first major study to challenge the work of John Neale.
Graves, M. *Elizabethan Parliaments, 1559–1601* (Longman, 1987) is a well-written revisionist study of Elizabeth and her Parliament with a useful section of documents.
Haigh, C. (ed.) *The Reign of Elizabeth I* (Macmillan, 1984) is a series of excellent essays.
Haigh, C. *Elizabeth I* (Longman, 1988) is not a traditional biography, but approaches Elizabeth's reign through a study of her exercise of power. It examines how she wielded the limited power she possessed.
Neale, J. *Queen Elizabeth I* (Penguin, 1960) is still the classic biography of Elizabeth, although it tends to be rather uncritical and nationalist.
Neale, J. *The Elizabethan House of Commons* (Cape, 1949) gives the traditional view of conflict between Elizabeth and Parliament.
Starkey, D. *Elizabeth* (Chatto and Windus, 2000) is a wonderful introduction to Elizabeth and sheds light on the influence her arly years had on later actions.
am, R.B. *Before the Armada: the Growth of English Foreign icy 1485–1588* (Cape, 1966) covers the early part of the reign some detail.
am, R.B. *The Making of Elizabethan Foreign Policy* ersity of California Press, 1980) provides students with a amount of detail.
son, C. *Queen Elizabeth and the Revolt of the Netherlands* (Macmillan, 1970) is a detailed study of one crucial aspect of Elizabeth's foreign policy.

Index